Published in 1996 by
Bluewood Books
A Division of The Siyeh Group, Inc.,
38 South B Street, Suite 202
San Mateo, CA 94401

ISBN 0-912517-22-0

Printed in the USA

Edited by Barbara Krystal

Designed by Bill Yenne
with the help of Azia Yenne.

Proofread by Joan Hayes

Key to front cover illustration: The main picture is Charles Lindbergh. Clockwise from Lindbergh are: Fridtjof Nansen, Alan Shepard, Valentina Tereshkova, Hernando De Soto, Henry Morton Stanley and Christopher Columbus.

The illustrations in this book are by Tony Chikes, with the following exceptions:
AGS Archives: 11 (top), 13 (top), 16, 17, 21, 24, 26, 30, 31, 32, 48, 51, 53, 55, 58 (bottom), 59 (bottom), 61 (bottom), 63, 64 (bottom), 65 (bottom), 69, 71, 73 (bottom), 74 (bottom), 83
National Aeronautics & Space Administration: 86-92, 94-97, 99-100, 103 (top), 104
© Chris Peterson: 58 (top), 64 (top)

100 EXPLORERS

WHO SHAPED WORLD HISTORY

Jerome Prescott

A Bluewood Book

TABLE OF CONTENTS

22. 23. 24. 25. 26.
18. 19. 20. 21.
9. 10. 11. 12. 13. 14. 15. 16. 17.
1. 2. 3. 4. 5. 6. 7. 8.

500 BC 1500 AD

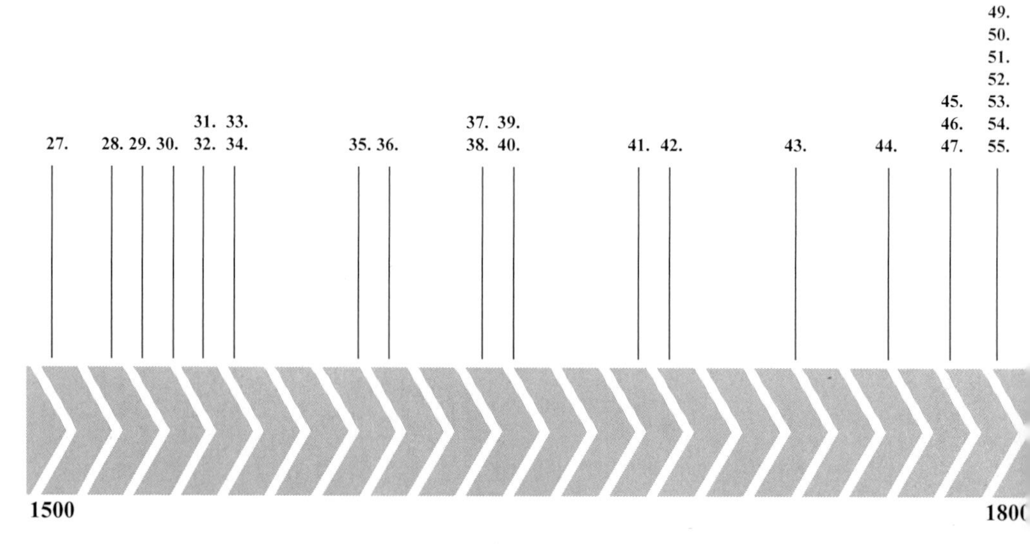
27.
28. 29. 30.
31. 32.
33. 34.
35. 36.
37. 38.
39. 40.
41. 42.
43.
44.
45. 46. 47.
48. 49. 50. 51. 52. 53. 54. 55.
1500

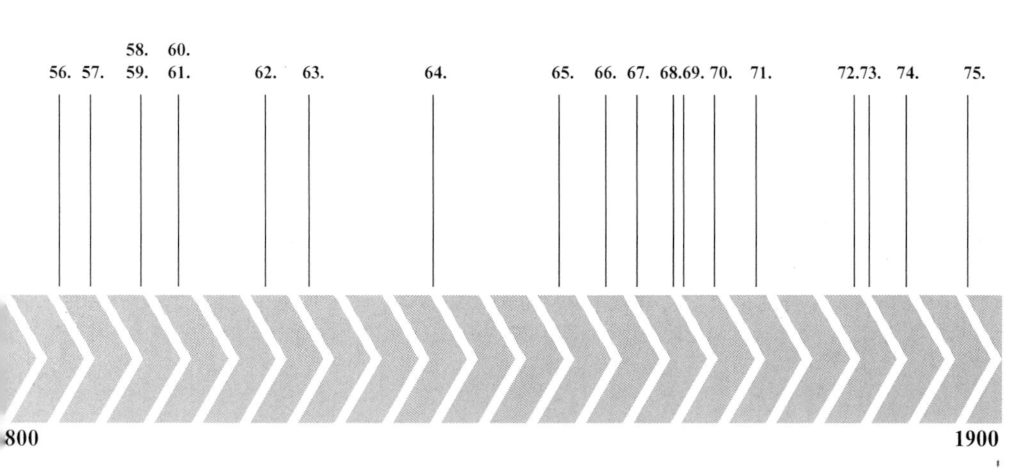
58. 60.
56. 57. 59. 61. 62. 63. 64. 65. 66. 67. 68.69. 70. 71. 72.73. 74. 75.
800
1900

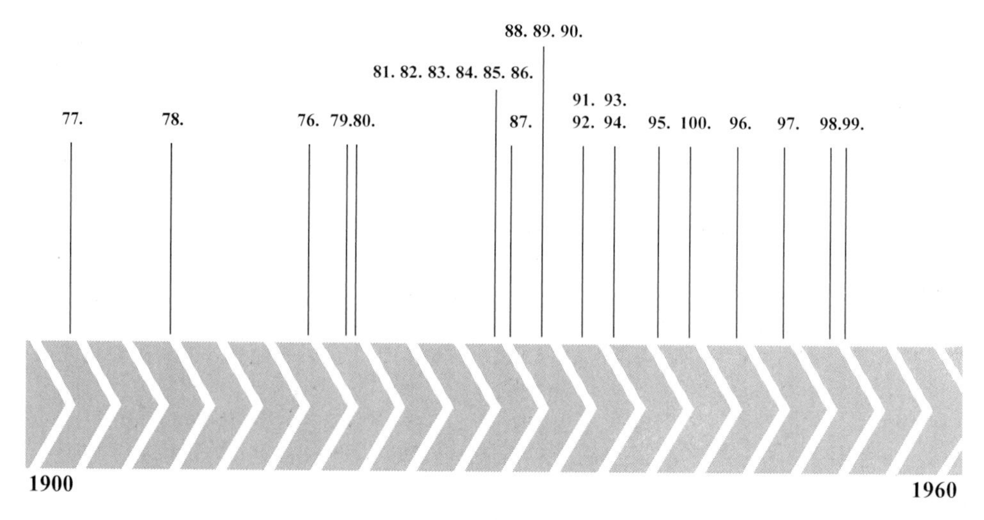
88. 89. 90.
81. 82. 83. 84. 85. 86.
91. 93.
77.
78.
76. 79.80.
87.
92. 94.
95. 100.
96.
97.
98.99.
1900
1960

INTRODUCTION

The earliest maps were rough sketches of an unknown world made by the wisest of our ancestors. The geographer of those days was like a traveller who stands at night in an unknown place holding a flickering lantern that casts a little circle of light near his feet. Outside this circle is a vast darkness that holds many mysteries. The imagination paints many of these as unknown terrors. The map makers of old called this area "*terra incognita*," or literally "unknown land."

Today, the "*terra incognita*," mysterious blank areas on the maps, are nearly all filled in. This process took many centuries and the lives of many brave explorers.

Until well into the middle of the twentieth century, maps were made by surveyors who literally had to travel across the land they were mapping and go where few people had gone before.

The few that had gone before were the explorers. Between the tenth and thirteenth centuries, tenuous expeditions linked the heart of Europe with that of Asia. European explorers wintered in North America, although they did not realize where they were.

The dawn of the sixteenth century saw the beginning of the "Age of Exploration." Europeans began to systematically explore and map the east coast of the Western Hemisphere and to open the sea lanes to Asia by way of Africa. At the beginning of the sixteenth century, virtually no one in Europe could comprehend the existence of a Western Hemisphere and no European had ever sailed to India by way of the southern tip of Africa. At the beginning of the seventeenth century there were regular trade routes in place that linked Europe to both America and Asia; and European colonies existed in what had earlier been *terra incognita*. Before the colonists and the commercial ships had come the explorers with their dreams of new horizons.

At the dawn of the twentieth century, nobody had set foot at either of the Earth's poles. Within 11 years, flags flew at both. The twentieth century was a new "Age of Exploration." Not only were the poles reached, humans had also descended nearly seven miles into the deepest ocean and twelve men had walked upon the moon.

This is the story of 100 of the brave souls who pushed back the daunting curtain of *terra incognita*. Included are those who organized the first expeditions to North America and the first expeditions around the world. We include the stories of the men who competed to be the first to set foot at the poles and those who died trying.

Among the 100 are the first man and the first woman to fly solo across one of the world's oceans and the first man and woman to fly in outer space. Also included are the heroic twelve who walked on the lunar surface, the pair who set a record for deep sea depth, the pair who flew around the world non-stop, and the only man who climbed the world's 14 tallest mountains without oxygen.

This book is a celebration of the indomitable human spirit and the curiosity that has always driven us to venture bravely into the unknown.

HERODOTUS

485-425 BC

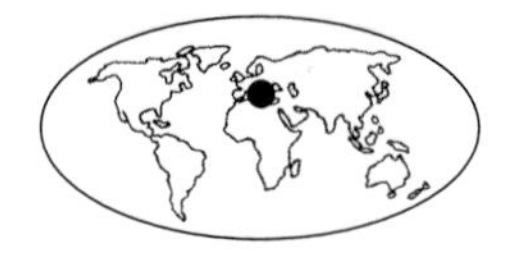

Best known as the first great historian, **Herodotus** was also an explorer. He travelled widely in the Mediterranean region at a time when people didn't venture far from home. Those who did were more interested in specific trading relationships than in recording a detailed account of distant places. Indeed, the historical work of Herodotus was based on his own field studies. Born in Halicarnassus in Asia Minor (now Turkey), he may have played an important part in the revolution at Halicarnassus in which the tyrant Lygdamis was overthrown. He himself was subsequently exiled.

The main subject of his historical writing was the war between Persia and Greece, which he saw as the final battles of a struggle that had been going on for centuries between the East and the West. Herodotus had a theory of history that was partly philosophical, partly theological, and the facts are marshaled and interpreted in this way. The theory was a modification of the old Greek belief in "the golden mean." Whatever exceeded a just proportion was supposed to excite the envy of the gods, and to bring with it punishment and disaster.

The work of Herodotus contains much that is derived from popular legend and is an invaluable storehouse of ancient folklore, which makes it a valuable resource for cultural historians.

However, a key element in the value of his work was that he actually explored the regions about which he wrote. Where more than one version of an event had come down to him, he used the version that best illustrated his theory of the working of destiny. He borrowed accounts of historical events from his predecessors without acknowledgment, in accordance with the general custom of the day, but he also based his work on his own observations and research. Wherever he is describing his own experiences he is thoroughly trustworthy.

Herodotus travelled extensively, not only through the city states of Greece, but in Asia Minor (now Turkey) and the Middle East. In many cases, his accounts of these latter places were the first detailed accounts to be circulated in Greece.

He lived for a many years in Athens and took part in the foundation of the colony of Thurii in southern Italy, where he probably died.

Herodotus.

2. XENOPHON
430-355 BC

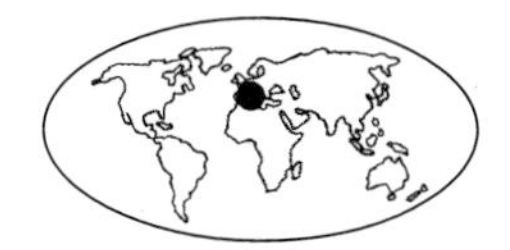

Xenophon was a Greek historian whose work was based on what he learned during his own explorations. Born in Erchia, Attica, Xenophon studied in Athens, where he was a disciple of **Socrates**. In 401 BC Xenophon joined the Greek corps recruited by **Cyrus the Younger** for a campaign against Artaxerxes II of Persia. Amid the confusion that followed the death of Cyrus in the Battle of Cunaxa, Xenophon was elected to lead the Greeks in their retreat to the Euxine. His most notable work,

The Anabasis, also called "The Retreat of the Ten Thousand," describes the plights and exploits of the Greeks during their 1,000-mile march through Assyria and Armenia to the sea.

With many of his followers, Xenophon joined the army of Agesilius, king of Sparta. After serving in Asiatic military campaigns, Xenophon fought against the Athenian allies in the Battle of Coronea (394 BC). As a result, he was consequently banished from Athens.

Xenophon.

Besides *The Anabasis*, his principal historical work is *The Hellenica,* or *History of Greece*, a continuation of the work of Thucydides. *Hellenica* is important not only for its historical facts, but also for its accounts of places that Xenophon visited in the course of his military campaigns and other expeditions. He explored areas as far away as Cunaxa, in what is now Iraq, and he was in Persia during his campaigns with Cyrus. His narratives on Persia were the first detailed accounts to reach Greece.

Rewarded by the Spartans with an estate at Scillus, near Olympia, he led a leisurely life until 370 BC, when he was driven out by the Eleans. He subsequently lived in Corinth, but is supposed to have returned to Athens before his death. Xenophon's works are admired for their vivid detail and simple, candid style, and for his vivid descriptions of places in the Middle East about which the average Spartan or Athenian knew little or nothing.

3. ST. BRENDAN
484-587AD

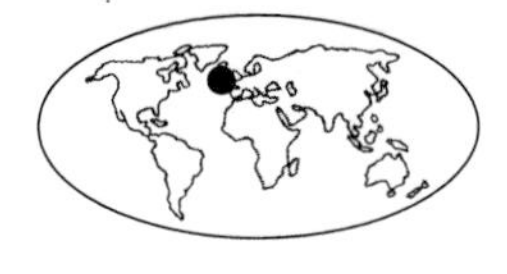

The Irish cleric who may have been the first European to sail to and from North America, **Brendan** was born in Tralee, Ireland. At the age of six he was sent to St. Jarlath's monastic school in Taum, where he remained until he was ordained by St. Erc in 512 AD. He founded several monasteries in Ireland, including the important one at Clonfert, which he started in 559 as a center of missionary activity.

St. Brendan made missionary voyages himself, travelling to England and Scotland, as well as around Ireland. His most important trip, however, was his voyage to "the Land of Promise," which he described in great detail in his epic saga *Navgatio Sancti Brendani Abbatis (The Navigations of the Abbot, St. Brendan).*

The narrative was translated into several languages and widely distributed in Europe during the Middle Ages. It tells how St. Brendan constructed a hide-covered *curragh* (boat) and sailed from the west of Ireland to Iceland and Greenland, to Newfound-land, and ultimately back to Ireland. The details of his descriptions of the specific landmarks and distances between those landmarks was very precise.

For several centuries after the close of the Middle Ages, scholars regarded St. Brendan's tales as interesting, but improbable fiction. However, in 1976-1977, **Tim Severin,** an experienced sailor and expert on the history of exploration, decided to resolve the question. Severin constructed a *curragh* to fifth century specifications and, using St. Brendan's narrative as his guide, set out to duplicate the voyage. Severin succeeded in reaching Newfoundland via Iceland and Greenland, and returned to Ireland having proven that it was possible to cross the Atlantic using fifth century technology. He also confirmed that details of St. Brendan's account were accurate for someone making such a journey in such a vessel.

St. Brendan.

Brendan had undertaken his voyage out of a combination of curiosity and a desire to fulfill the Church's belief that the the words of the scriptures should be taken to the "ends of the Earth." Brendan sought to find those "ends," and found new lands that his contemporaries found hard to imagine.

4.5. ERIC THE RED and LIEF ERICSON
c. 950 AD, c.1000 AD

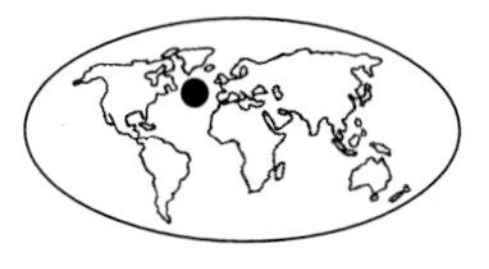

The history of exploration includes a number of instances where both father and son did important work. The Polos and the Cabots certainly come to mind, but few such duos are more colorful than the Norwegian discoverers and colonizers **Eric the Red** and his son **Lief Ericson**. Wherever the sagas of the great dragon-headed Viking ships and their fearless crews are recalled, the names Eric and Lief are spoken with justified respect.

Eric was the son of the great Norwegian chief **Thorvald**. Exiled from Norway for manslaughter, both father and son went to Iceland, where Thorvald died. Eric married and lived for a time in Iceland. Outlawed for murder, he started on a voyage of discovery and reached Greenland, where he remained for three winters. He then returned to Iceland to obtain people to start a new colony in Greenland. It is said that he picked the name as a public relations gimmick to imply that Greenland was actually "green." Eric chose to establish a new colony in Greenland partly to escape Norway, where he and his father had been in trouble, partly out of a seaman's urge to experience the lands beyond the horizon. There was also a religious element. Lief is said to have gone from Greenland to Norway, where he was converted to Christianity, and to have brought a Christian priest back with him to Greenland. As such, he was instrumental in Christianizing Greenland.

Eric the Red.

Lief Ericson.

In about 1000 AD, Lief sailed from Greenland to search for the "new land to the west," which **Bjarni Herjulfson** had sighted in 986. He found such a place, and went ashore. Lief Ericson and his crew wintered in a place which they called **Vinland**. The site of this landfall and winter-quarters have been variously identified as Labrador, Newfoundland, and Nova Scotia, although there are Viking archeological remains as far south as the New England coast.

6. MARCO POLO
1254?-1324

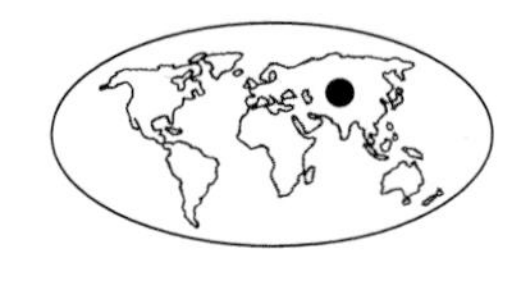

Marco Polo was born in the Italian city-state of Venice at a time when Europeans had little or no idea of the people and cultures of China and east Asia. Europeans had heard that China existed, but knew little about Asia beyond what they had heard about **Genghis Khan** and his Mongol Hordes or what they had learned second-hand from traders who had travelled in Turkey or the Middle East.

In 1271, Marco accompanied his father and uncle, **Nicolo Polo** and **Maffeo Polo** on a trip to China. Their theory of exploration was that the the best way to learn about this land to the east was to go there. In fact, the older Polos had been to China on an expedition in 1269. For Marco, however, the trip would be more than merely the reconnaissance of a trader. Marco was more interested in learning what he could about China and its people.

After a long journey, the Polo party was received at the royal court of China's Mongol emperor, **Kublai Khan (1215-1294)**, who took a liking to Marco. The emperor, who was very interested in European culture, found in Marco, a European who was fascinated with China. Kublai Khan made the young man his ambassador at large, sending him on many missions within China, as well as to Tibet and Burma. Eventually, Marco Polo saw more of Asia than any European had ever seen, or even had dreamed of seeing. Along with his father and uncle, he stayed in China for over 20 years, learning the languages and customs of Asia and meeting many of its diverse peoples.

When the Polos returned to Venice in 1295, they were met with skepticism. After they demonstrated what they had learned in China, their fellow Venetians were quite impressed, and the Polos were welcomed and honored. Many of the things that they had brought back from China were truly amazing and had never been seen in Europe before. These included exquisite silks, as well as technology not widely known outside China, such as gunpowder. There is even an unproven tale that they introduced spaghetti into Italy from China.

The difficulty of traveling over land made trade between Europe and the Far East slow to develop. Marco Polo published the details of a workable trade route. His travels of discovery expanded Europe's horizons beyond anything most people could ever have imagined possible. Indeed, the voyages of **Christopher Columbus** (see No. 11) two centuries later were also inspired by the desire to find a shorter, easier route to the riches of China.

Marco's book, *The Travels of Marco Polo*, is perhaps the most famous and influential travel book in history. With its wealth of detail, it provided Europeans of the Middle Ages with their first substantial knowledge of China and other Asian countries.

Marco Polo.

7. HENRY THE NAVIGATOR
1394-1460

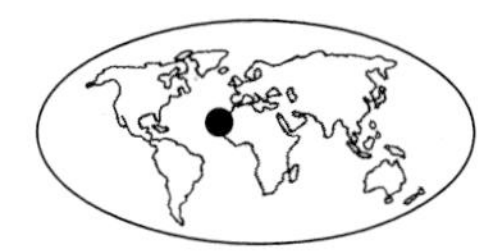

In the early part of the fifteenth century, even before the birth of **Christopher Columbus** (see No. 11), there was an interest in systematically exploring the mysteries beyond the western horizon. It was still generally accepted that the world was flat, but there were rumors that islands existed out beyond what was visible to the naked eye.

A vessel on the high seas.

Prince Henry, known as "the Navigator," was the son of John I, king of Portugal, and Philippa, sister of Henry IV of England. After showing conspicuous courage at the siege of Ceuta in 1415, he devoted himself to the development of navigation and the fostering of maritime expeditions.

Maritime trade was a competitive enterprise and one that was of vital interest to a small country such as Portugal, so the discovery of new trade routes was an important objective of exploration for Henry.

In 1440, he reached Cape Blanco, and in 1446, he landed in the Cape Verde Islands. Henry dropped anchor in the Azores in 1448. Actually "discovered" in 1431 by another Portuguese seaman, **Pedro Alvares Cabral** (see No. 15), the Azores are nearly 900 miles west of continental Europe.

Prince Henry of Portugal, the Navigator.

In the Azores, Henry the Navigator built an observatory. He also established an important navigation school at Sagres, near Cape St. Vincent in southern Portugal. He did not, however, live to see the fabulous discoveries that would be made at the close of the fifteenth century, when the Spanish and Portuguese sailed to discover a new world.

8.9. VINCENTE and MARTIN PINZON
1440-1493, 1460-1524

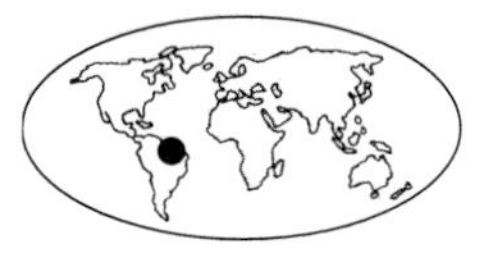

Often overlooked in the stories of the great explorers are those who were present for the discovery, but who are not recorded because all the glory went to the man in charge. Such was the case of two brothers, **Martin Alonzo Pinzon** and **Vincente Yanez Pinzon.**

They were born in Palos, members of a wealthy family of shipbuilders.and later sailed with **Christopher Columbus** (see No.11).

Martin Pinzon helped to finance and equip Columbus' three ships for his first voyage of discovery. In 1492 received command of the *Pinta*. His brother **Francisco Pinzon** was also aboard as his pilot. In fact, it was Martin Pinzon who suggested the alteration in course that brought the ships to San Salvador in the Bahamas on October 12, 1492.

A month later, Pinzon's *Pinta* became separated from Columbus' *Santa Maria.* Pinzon wanted to precede his commander in discovering gold and in reporting the success of the expedition in Spain. Pinzon landed at Haiti in December 1492, and it was here that Columbus found him in January 1493.

The ships were separated again on the return voyage, and Martin Pinzon reached Galicia in February 1493. Having landed, he dispatched what was the first report of the new discoveries.

Columbus arrived in Palos in March and his report actually reached the Spanish monarchs first.

Vincente Pinzon also accompanied Columbus on his 1492 first voyage to the New World, commanding the *Nina*. Unlike Martin, however, Vincente made no attempt to rival Columbus with his tales of discovery. Later, he surveyed much of the Caribbean basin, for which he received credit, if not the sort of renown that Columbus would enjoy.

On a voyage of his own in 1499-1500 Vincente Pinzon discovered the mouth of the Amazon River in what is now Brazil. He proceeded north to present-day Costa Rica, returning to Spain via Haiti and the Bahama Islands. In two later voyages, which were conducted in 1507 and 1508-1509, Vincente sailed with Juan Diaz de Solis. During the 1508-1509 voyage, Vincente Pinzon sailed along the east coast of Central and South America, probably reaching as far south as what is now southern Argentina. Records of Vincente Pinzon's life cease mysteriously in 1523, when he was in living back in Palos.

Although they are in the shadow of Columbus, the Pinzons sailed farther and added much more to European knowledge of the Western Hemisphere.

Vincente Pinzon and his brother, Martin Pinzon.

10. GIOVANNI CABOTO
1450-1498

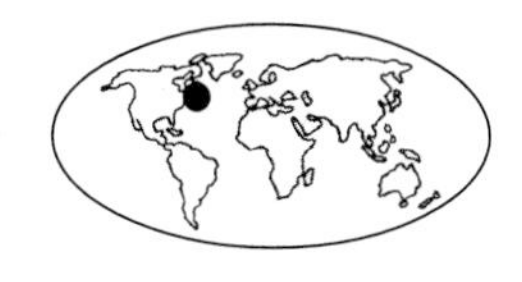

Giovanni Caboto is best remembered for the work he did while employed by the English under the anglicized name **John Cabot**. As a naturalized citizen of Venice, Caboto sailed to the eastern-most parts of the Mediterranean. He was a commercial seaman who had visited Mecca and had seen the incoming caravans from India laden with spices and gems.

It was under the English flag that Cabot is credited as being the first European to set foot on the North American mainland. He might have sailed to America for Venice, but England had deeper coffers. While it is now known that **Lief Ericson**'s expedition, (see No. 5) and almost certainly **St. Brendan** (see No. 3) accomplished this ahead of Caboto, he was the first in the Columbus-era wave of discovery, and it was his landing that led directly to English colonization a century later.

He believed, as **Christopher Columbus** (see No.11) did, that the Far East might be reached by sailing to the westward. With this notion he soon moved to England, on the invitation of King Henry VII, who had read his resume and liked what he saw. The news of what the Spanish were finding in the "New World" was taking Europe by storm, and Henry wanted a navigator who could get England a piece of the action. Under Henry VII's flag, Caboto sailed in the ship *Matthew* from Bristol in 1497. Among the crew were John Cabot's three sons **Lewis, Sebastian** (see No. 20) and **Santius**.

On St. John's Day in June 1497, they reached Labrador. They were the first Europeans in five centuries to set foot on the mainland continental mass of North America.

Indeed, another 14 months elapsed before Columbus himself touched the mainland. Two years would pass before Vespucci traced the shore of South America. It was on June 24 that he landed on Cape Breton Island (now part of the Canadian province of Nova Scotia) and took possession of it for the king.

Although it was summer, Cabot found the country which he had discovered to be ice-bound and wrapped in the solitude of an apparently perpetual winter. The coast was forbidding, but a few Native Americans did come to see their ship. The shoreline was explored for several hundred miles, and Cabot imagined that he had found the kingdom of China, although the terrain that he saw and the people he met did not match what was known in Europe about China. The king was impressed with the story, and when he returned to Bristol in 1497, the king issued a new, more generous, commission, hoping that Caboto would find a lucrative trading port. In his second voyage in 1498, Caboto explored the coast of Greenland and sailed south as far as the area around Chesapeake Bay.

After 1498, the name of John Cabot disappears from the record. Where the remainder of his life was passed and the circumstances of his death are unknown, though he probably perished on the second voyage.

Giovanni Caboto (John Cabot).

11. CHRISTOPHER COLUMBUS
1451-1506

The once much-applauded, now much-maligned, Italian explorer did not "discover" America; nor did he confirm that the world was not flat. **Christopher Columbus** did, however, succeed in placing the Western Hemisphere permanently in the consciousness of Western Europe. He began the chain of events that would lead to European colonization, and later domination, of the Western Hemisphere.

Born in Genoa, the great Italian seaport, **Christoforo Colombo** (in Spanish, **Cristobal Colon**) went to sea at the age of 14 on the Mediterranean.

He was wrecked during a fight with some Venetian galleys off the coast of Portugal in 1470, and settled in Lisbon. During the next few years he made many voyages to Madeira and the Azores. He became convinced that it was possible to reach India by sailing west. After making a vain appeal to the government of Genoa, he turned to the King of Portugal, but without result. He went to Henry VII of England and to the dukes of Medina Sidonia and Medina Celi, who suggested that he try **Queen Isabella** of Castile in Spain. She was convinced to finance his scheme.

On August 3, 1492, Columbus set sail with three ships, the *Nina*, the *Pinta*, and the *Santa Maria.* They sailed west until, after much trepidation and a near-mutiny, they spotted land on October 12.

The expedition disembarked and took possession of a small island in the Bahamas which Columbus called San Salvador. Columbus explored Cuba on October 28 and named Hispaniola (now Haiti and the Dominican Republic) a little more than a month later. On January 4, 1493, with the *Santa Maria* having been wrecked, the expedition set sail for Europe. Columbus dropped anchor at Palos on March 15, 1493.

When he strode into the Spanish court bearing the fruits of the discoveries, Columbus was received with great honor and fanfare. A second expedition of 17 vessels and 1,500 men was immediately fitted out and placed at his command. If Columbus' motivation was primarily the mariner's interest in finding a trade route, the Spanish government was motivated by the potential wealth that would come from the discovery of that trade route.

The second expedition sailed in September 1493, and reached the island of Dominica in the West Indies on November 3. After two years spent in exploration of the newly discovered islands, including the island of Jamaica, discovered May 14, 1494, and an attempt at colonization, Columbus returned to Spain, reaching Cadiz in June 1496.

A third fleet of six vessels was fitted out, and on May 30, 1498, the explorer sailed

Christopher Columbus.

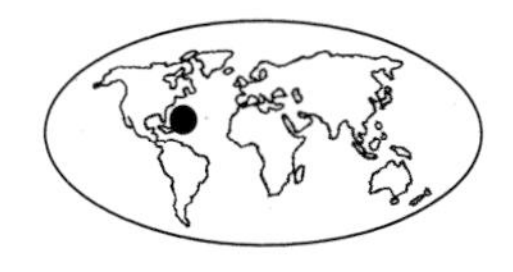

for what would turn out to be the mainland of South America.

Arrested for "interference" by **Francisco de Bobadilla**, the newly-appointed royal governor of Hispaniola, Columbus was sent back to Spain in irons. He was, however, restored to favor by the king and queen, and was given a fourth fleet. He embarked in 1502, on his last voyage, where he explored the south shore of the Gulf of Mexico.

Columbus returned to Spain in 1504, having become ill in the Caribbean, and two years later, on May 20, 1506, he died at Valladolid. His influence on the islands where he landed was minimal, but Columbus had opened the door for others whose effect would be profound. They would come to build forts, spread disease, and plunder. Within a generation, the "new lands" were a very changed place. Columbus was the practical navigator and able seaman whose vision of a new route to the Indies led him to the discovery of the New World. The results were the opening of an era of exploration and colonization never equaled before or since, and the spread of Western civilization to two new continents.

There is the myth that Columbus' scheme was rejected by the learned men of the **College of Salamanca** because he could not convince them the earth was round. Actually, however, the Salamanca commission did not question Columbus' ideas about the shape of the earth, but his contention that the ocean separating Europe and the Indies was only half as wide as the current belief held it to be. There was no turning back, though, Columbus had inspired a new generation of explorers.

A somewhat glamorized view of Christopher Columbus landing at San Salvador.

12. BARTHOLOMEU DIAZ
1450-1500

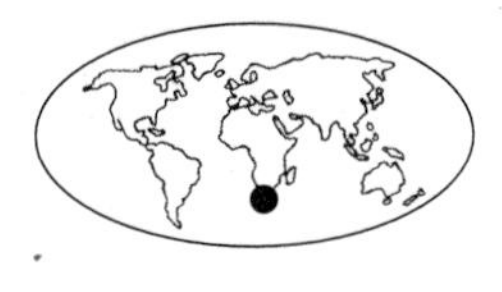

Born near Lisbon, **Bartholomeu Diaz** grew up around boats and had proved himself to be a gifted navigator and a natural seaman. He lived in an era when Portugal was one of the world's foremost maritime powers and all around him were the men who'd sailed with **Henry the Navigator** (see No.7) and the great **Diego Cao.**

The stories that circulated on the docks at Lisbon told of Henry's voyages to the island's beyond the horizon and Cao's expedition south along the coast of Africa. Cao, who died in 1486, had explored as far south as the mouth of the Congo (now Zaire) River by 1484.

Bartholomeu Diaz was anxious to see what was around the next bend in that coastline. This sense of eagerness for exploration hade him a natural choice for Portugal's King John II, when he needed a good seaman to command two vessels to push the envelope of Cao's discoveries along the west coast of Africa.

The king wanted to see Portugal stay competitive in the world of international trade and imagined that one way to do that was to be the first to open a new trade route. The route south was attractive, because the Spanish were not yet active there and Portugal had a head start.

Diaz sailed south and rounded the southern end of Africa without immediately realizing the fact. He discovered Algoa Bay and continuing farther, noted the northeasterly swing of the coast. Only then did he realize that Africa had been rounded.

He named the most southern point the Cape of Storms, but King John changed it to the Cape of Good Hope, which it remains today. The crew became nervous and convinced Diaz to return to Lisbon. Later Diaz sailed with Vasco da Gama, who had superseded him as leader, to the Cape Verde Islands. He joined **Pedro Alvares Cabral**'s expedition (see No. 15), which discovered Brazil, but he was lost in a storm on the return voyage in 1500.

One member of Diaz's Cape of Good Hope crew was of particular note; **Bartholomew Columbus** (1445-1515), the much lesser-known brother of **Christopher Columbus**, may have possibly accompanied Bartholomeu Diaz on his voyage to the Cape of Good Hope.

As for Bartholomeu Diaz, he had, in charting the course to the Cape of Good Hope, opened the door for future Portuguese navigators, who would use that route to open trade with India.

Bartholomeu Diaz.

13. AMERIGO VESPUCCI
1454-1512

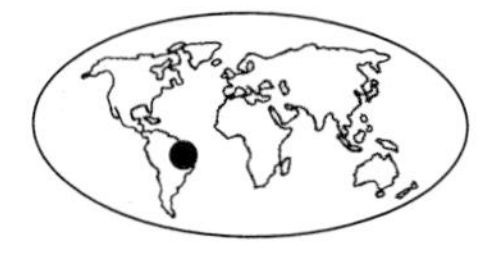

Born in land-locked Florence, Italy, **Amerigo Vespucci** is best remembered as the namesake of the two continents of the Western Hemisphere. He did, however, participate in several voyages to the Western Hemisphere.

Vespucci was one of those who followed quickly in the wake of the early discoveries. He signed on for his first voyage to the continent that bears his name with **Vincente Pinzon** (see No. 8) in 1497. In 1499 he sailed again, this time to the coast of South America, though the results of his voyage were not significant.

In 1501 he made another voyage, and returned to Europe to publish the first general account of the discoveries made in the Western World. A fourth voyage was made in 1503, and in 1508, he was made Pilot Major of Spain.

It was the wide circulation of his written accounts of his voyages which led to his name being associated with the actual discovery. The credit for the naming of "America" goes to the German geographer **Martin Waldseemuller** (1470-1513), who read these accounts, possibly too quickly. Eager to produce a new map quickly, Waldseemuller named the land mass for Amerigo Vespucci, whom he believed to have been the first discoverer. In his *Cosmographie Introductio in Super Quatuor Amerigo Vespucci Navigationis* (1507) he praised Vespucci and named America (some interpretations insist only *South* America) for the Florentine.

Although Waldseemuller later corrected his error and credited **Christopher Columbus** (see No. 11), the name stuck and later efforts to rename the continent "Columbia," have failed.

He became the new continent's erroneous namesake, but what of value did Vespucci actually accomplish? It was he who established the fact that the new islands and mainland on the western shores of the Atlantic were not the East Indies, but were indeed another continent.

Amerigo Vespucci. Waldseemuller originally thought he discovered America.

14. JUAN PONCE DE LEON
1460-1521

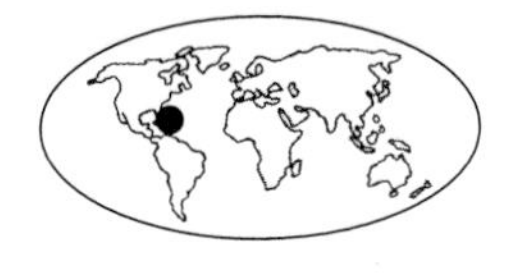

The Spanish explorer of Florida, **Juan Ponce de León** is remembered best for his bizarre obsession with a mysterious "Fountain of Eternal Youth," for which he searched for years.

Born in San Servas, León in Spain, he served in the war against the Moors, and accompanied Columbus on his second voyage to America in 1493. Ponce de León also joined an expedition to Hispaniola in 1502, and commanded an expedition to Puerto Rico in 1508.

As the governor of Puerto Rico from 1510 to 1512, he was instrumental in founding San Juan in 1511. A rumor had circulated in the Spanish colonies that somewhere to the west, there was a land in which one might find a fountain of eternal youth, whose waters could prevent the aging process. The story appealed to the romantic sentiments of de León, and he set sail toward the land to the west.

De León reached a heretofore unexplored coast on Easter Sunday, 1513, and supposed that he had found a new island. The shores were covered with a luxuriant forest. The horizon across the bright waters was banked with green leaves. Birds were heard singing there, and the fragrance of blossoms was wafted to the ships.

The day on which the discovery was made was called in the calendar of the church Pascua Florida, or in Spanish, Pasqua de Flores. This notion caught the imagination of Ponce, and he named the new shore Florida, the Land of Flowers. A landing was made a few days later, near what is now of St. Augustine. The Spanish banner and arms were planted, and the country claimed for Spain by the right of discovery.

Ponce de León explored the Land of Flowers, continuing his search for the fountain of youth. He went about bathing in many waters up and down the coast before giving up the quest and sailing back to Puerto Rico. The law of nature had prevailed over tradition. He was no younger than before.

Nevertheless, the King of Spain appointed Ponce de León as governor of Florida, and ordered him to colonize the country. The old adventurer was slow in doing this, and it was nine years after the discovery before he returned to his province. He found there the usual results of Spanish colonial ignorance and cruelty.

In 1521, the Native Americans became hostile, attacked de León's colony, forcing them to run for their lives. In order to save themselves, they took to their ship and sailed away. Ponce de León himself was struck with an arrow, mortally wounded and taken to Cuba to die.

The discovery of Florida was of great importance, although it would be some time before it was determined that the Island of Flowers was not an island, but the mainland of North America.

Juan Ponce de León.

15.16. PEDRO CABRAL and JUAO CABRILLO 1460-1526, ?-1543

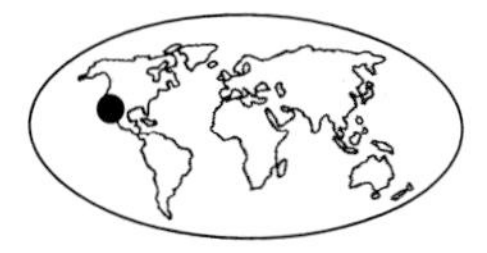

Portuguese colonization in the Western Hemisphere was minimal, but their accomplishments as navigators and explorers were remarkable. Two of the most renowned were a pair of men who learned the mariners' trade sailing from the same Lisbon docks, probably knew one another well, and who, between them, explored half the globe in the early sixteenth century.

In 1499 the king of Portugal placed **Pedro Alvares Cabral** (or Cabrera) in command of a fleet of 13 vessels with 1,200 men, bound for the East Indies. They took a course too far westerly, fell into the South American current of the Atlantic Ocean, and were carried to the unknown coast of Brazil.

Having claimed this land for Portugal, Cabral set a legacy that continues today. The 155 million people living in Brazil now constitute the largest Portuguese-speaking nation on Earth. Cabral was seeking adventure for himself and wealth for himself and for Portugal. With this in mind, he sailed for India, and landed at Mozambique, which he surveyed for the first time, and claimed. It would remain a Portuguese colony until 1975. Cabral reached Calicut and made the first, and very lucrative, commercial treaty between Portugal and India.

Cabral's colleague, **Juan (Juao) Rodriguez Cabrillo**, switched his allegiance to sail for the Spanish. While in the Western Hemisphere, he was sent by Viceroy **Antonio Mendoza** of Mexico to explore the west coast of North America in 1542. Cabrillo explored much of the coast of Southern California and followed the Pacific coast as far north as Oregon.

Today, place names from San Francisco to San Diego recall Cabillo's voyage, during which his expedition were the first Europeans to set foot on the Pacific shore of what is now the continental United States.

Juao (Juan) Rodriguez Cabrillo landing horses on the coast of central California.

17. TRISTAO (TRISTAN) DA CUNHA
1460-1540

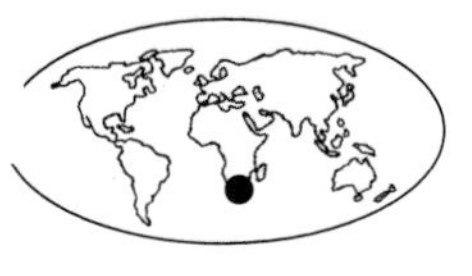

One of the most important of the Portuguese navigators was **Tristao (Tristan) da Cunha**. In 1506, while in command of a Portuguese expedition to Africa and India, he discovered in the South Atlantic the island which today bears his name, and which is the most remote inhabited island on Earth.

At the beginning of the sixteenth century, both Spain and Portugal operated huge fleets that were very active in exploration. The Spanish (or Italians working for the Spanish) were leading in the project of exploring the "new" lands to the west, the Portuguese were sailing south and east.

To understand the backdrop of the times when Da Cunha made his voyages, it is important to understand that at the beginning of the sixteenth century, Spain and Portugal began to contend for trade routes south and west. In 1493 the pope drew an imaginary vertical line in the Atlantic 300 miles west of the Azores.

All the islands and countries west of that meridian were given to Spain. Though the area had yet to be mapped, almost all of the New World — except present-day Brazil — lay in the Spanish zone. While this gave Portugal little to the west, Africa which was in the Portuguese zone. Indeed, Portugal kept and milked its African colonies for more than a century after Spain lost its American colonies.

Tristao da Cunha visited Madagascar, Mozambique, and the coast of Zanzibar. He distinguished himself in India, and in 1514, he headed a delegation to Rome to render homage to Pope Leo X for the territories newly conquered by the Portuguese.

Da Cunha became a celebrity in Portugal and retired to his estate near Lisbon in great comfort. He is also celebrated in song, specifically the tenth song of Camoens's *Os Lusiadas*.

Tristao (Tristan) da Cunha.

18. VASCO DA GAMA
1469?-1524

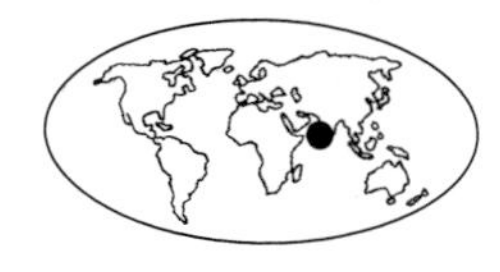

The Portuguese navigator who was the pioneer of European commerce and Portuguese commercial expansion in the Far East, **Vasco da Gama** was born at Sines in the province of Alentejo.

As both Spain and Portugal were sending out expeditions to find and secure important trade routes, da Gama was one of those who helped to stake Portugal's claim.

Chosen leader of an expedition to explore the east coast of Africa, Da Gama rounded the Cape of Good Hope in November 1497, reaching **Calicut** (not to be confused with Calcutta) on the Malabar coast of India in May 1498.

Da Gama had done what **Christopher Columbus** (see No. 11) had failed to do. He is credited with being the first European to discover a sea route to India. Although this would ultimately result in opening up commerce between East and West, his initial reception in Calicut was rather hostile, and he returned to Portugal in 1499.

In Portugal, his welcome was enthusiastic. The king recognized the tremendous economic importance, not only of a trade route around Africa, but of the new route all the way to the important commercial centers of Asia as well.

Vasco da Gama set out for India once more in 1502 with a powerfully well-armed fleet and bombarded Calicut into submission. Portugal established colonies and secured trading terms. Da Gama returned to his homeland in 1503 with valuable plunder, and 21 years later he was appointed viceroy of Portuguese India. However, he died the same year in Cochin China (later South Vietnam).

Like countryman **Tristao da Cunha** (see No. 17), da Gama is remembered in the epic, *Os Lusiados*, by Cameons. An account of his voyages, written by a companion, Alvaro Velho, was finally translated into English in 1898 as *A Journal of the Voyage of Vasco da Gama*.

Vasco da Gama succeeded in reaching the East Indies by sailing *west*.

19. FRANCISCO PIZZARO
1471-1541

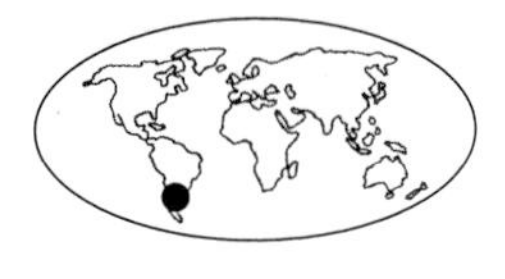

The explorers of the sixteenth century were characterized by their navigational daring and good will toward the lands they conquered. They were greedy, but also brave and often chivalrous. While the revisionist histories of the 1970s painted them as cruel villains, they were, in fact, just skilled navigators who were doing a job. They generally bore no particular ill feeling toward the native peoples.

A notable exception was **Francisco Pizzaro**, the cruel Spanish conquistador of Peru. He was born in Trujillo, Estremadura in Spain and sailed to America with the Oleda Expedition of 1509, where he helped Fernandez de Enciso found the town of Santa Maria la Antigua del Darien in Panama in 1510.

He was also a member of **Vasco de Balboa**'s party (see No. 21) when they "discovered" the Pacific Ocean in 1513. Having formed a partnership in Panama in 1522 with the adventurers **Diego de Almarco** and **Fernando de Luque**, Pizzaro set out to explore the wealthy land south of Panama.

He headed expeditions between 1524 and 1527, sailing as far south as the Gulf of Guayaquil. He came for gold and slaves. He found them, took them and brought them back from Native American settlements that he raided.

Pizzaro travelled to Spain with his plunder in 1528 to secure permission to conquer the Inca kingdom and to govern Peru. In 1531 he set out on this conquest. The following year he captured the Inca monarch, **Atahulpa,** at Cajamarca, and in 1533 executed him after having collected a tremendous ransom. Also in 1533, Pizzaro captured the Inca capital of Cuzco. He looted the Inca kingdom, stealing its treasure, killing its people and essentially destroying it as a cultural entity with his brutality.

Placing the Inca **Manco** on the throne as puppet ruler of Peru, with a Spanish guard to watch him, Pizzaro led his men to the Pacific Coast and founded the city of "Los Reyes" (present-day Lima), in 1535.

When he returned to Cuzco, he learned that Manco had led a native rebellion and was besieging that city.

The Spanish army brutally crushed the insurrection, but was soon involved in a new battle, this time with Pizzaro's partner Almarco, who had become governor of New Toledo (now Chile) and claimed disputed territory between the two countries. Almagro was defeated at Las Salinas in 1538 and executed. Three years later his avengers killed the bloodthirsty Pizzaro.

In 1548, his brother **Gonzalo Pizzaro,** led a revolt against the new viceroy of Peru, failed and was executed.

Francisco Pizzaro.

20. SEBASTIAN CABOT
1474-1557

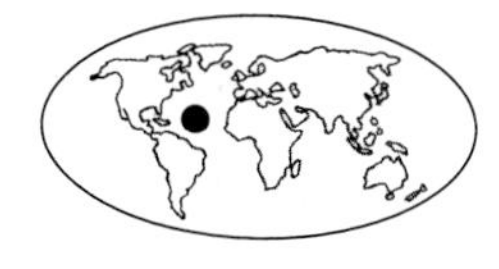

The second son of **Giovanni Caboto (John Cabot**, see No. 10), **Sebastian Cabot** inherited not only the plans and reputation of his father, but also his genius.

In 1498, Sebastian Cabot, at age 22, was placed in command of a flotilla of well-manned English vessels and on his way to the new continent.

The objective was to explore the areas south of where Sebastian's father had landed. The English wanted him to to ascertain whether there was commercial potential in this region, and if so, to take possession of the land in this area. The voyage of Sebastian proceeded well until he reached the seas west of Greenland. Here he was obliged by the icebergs to change his course.

The shore of Labrador was reached not far from the scene of his father's earlier landing, and Sebastian turned southward, across the Gulf of St. Lawrence, or to the east of Newfoundland. His expedition explored New Brunswick, Nova Scotia, and the coast of Maine. At Cape Hatteras, Sebastian began his homeward voyage. It was in this manner that the right of England to the better parts of North America was first declared.

Sebastian Cabot.

This first view was called "discovery," and the kings of Europe had agreed among themselves that "discovery" would constitute a right which they would mutually respect and defend. All the claims of the Native Americans were brushed aside as not of consequence or validity. Thanks to Sebastian Cabot's having landed here, England felt that it now had a right to the possession of the continent thus "discovered."

As for Sebastian Cabot himself, his future career was as strange as his voyages had been wonderful. The dark minded Henry VII, although quick to appreciate the value of Cabot's discoveries, was slow to reward the discoverer. Cabot's accomplishments did not go unnoticed elsewhere. Ferdinand the Catholic, husband of Isabella, patron of Columbus, enticed Sebastian Cabot away from England and made him Pilot Major of Spain.

Unlike his father, who sailed for the English crown, Sebastian Cabot was in the service of Spain almost continuously from 1512 to 1548, being Pilot Major most of the time. In 1525, Cabot commanded an expedition which explored the coast of Brazil and the La Plata River.

On his return to Spain in 1530, however, he got into a disagreement with members of the court and was banished to Oran, in what is now Morocco. He was later reinstated as Pilot Major. Arriving in England after 1548, he was given a pension by Edward VI. In 1553 he was the director of an expedition of Merchant Adventurers which opened to England an important commerce with Russia.

21. VASCO NUNEZ DE BALBOA
1475-1517

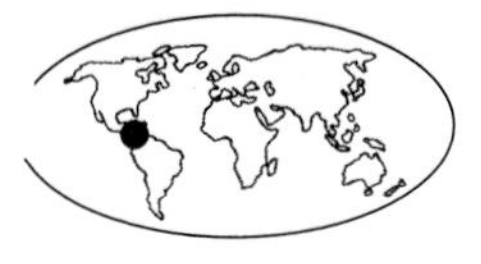

The Spanish explorer credited with being the first European to lead an expedition to the shores of the Pacific Ocean, **Vasco Nuñez de Balboa** was born in Jere de los Caballeros, Spain and accompanied Rodrigo Bastidas to Central America in 1500. Through spending, borrowing and/or gambling, Balboa ran up some debts. To escape his creditors, he joined the 1510 expedition being sent to relieve the settlement of San Sebastian, which was being besieged by Native Americans.

Finding the colony in ruins, Balboa suggested founding the town that would be known as Santa Maria del Antigua del Darien (Antigua), of which he became the *alcalde* (mayor). He later expanded his office to become governor of Darien (Panama). Hearing that he was in disfavor with the king, he was determined to raise his image by exploring and claiming new lands for the crown.

Balboa wades in the Pacific, September 29, 1513.

Balboa had learned from the native people that a "great water" lay not far to the west, so in September 1513, he set out with a large force to cross the mountains and verify the story of this great ocean on the other side of the isthmus. On September 25, from a high peak, he was the first European to see the eastern waters of the Pacific Ocean. On September 29, carrying in his hand the banner of Spain, he waded in. In the pompous fashion of his age, and with drawn sword and flourish, he took possession of what he named Mar del Sur (southern sea) and formally claimed it and the lands washed by it for King Ferdinand.

He was awarded the title of "Admiral of the Southern Sea," but was superseded by Pedro Arias de Avila as governor. Vasco Nuñez de Balboa's later expeditions caused the jealousy of de Avila, who had him arrested on an apparently unfounded charge of treason. He was convicted and executed.

22. FERDINAND MAGELLAN
1480-1521

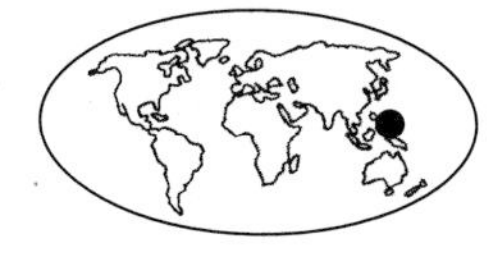

Born in Sabrosa, Portugal, **Fernao de Magalhaes** (in Spanish, **Ferdinand Magellan**) was the navigator and explorer who launched the expedition that proved conclusively that the Earth is round. Early in his career, he served ably in the West Indies. At this time, it was clear that although **Christopher Columbus** (see No. 11) had found a new continent, he had failed to find a western route to the East Indies. Magalhaes tried, but failed, to interest the Portuguese government in financing a voyage to accomplish what Columbus had not. He offered his idea and his services to Charles V of Spain, who accepted.

On September 20, 1519, "Magellan" set sail from Spain with five ships to sail, essentially, around the world. Since no one had found a route through the center of the Western Hemisphere, he decided to sail around its southern edge. He travelled southwest and reached landfall near present-day Buenos Aires, Argentina, by mid-October. He followed the coastline south and discovered a passage—albeit a cold and rugged 360-mile trip—around the tip of South America on October 21. This passage, which connects the Atlantic and Pacific oceans, ever afterward was known as the **Straits of Magellan**, one of the roughest stretches of water on Earth. Magellan called it Todos los Santos. During the days of sailing ships and before the Panama Canal was built, the straits were widely used. Today it is still the favored passage for ships rounding South America.

When Magellan emerged from the straits, he dubbed the relatively peaceful waters he encountered the "Pacific" Ocean. Sailing across the long, open stretches of the Pacific Ocean left the sailors short of food, and they landed in the **Marianas Islands** to take supplies aboard. The expedition arrived in the Philippines in April 1521, where Magellan himself was killed in a fight with the natives on April 27.

With two remaining ships the survivors sailed though the East Indies. Only one ship, the *Vittoria,* under the command of Juao Sebastian del Cano, completed the voyage around the Cape of Good Hope and up the western coast of Africa. The survivors reached Seville early in September 1522. At the time of Magellan's death, he had essentially completed his task. He had travelled west around the world and reached waters then familiar to navigators sailing east.

The story of this history-making feat was told by **Antonio Pigafetta**, one of the Magellan's sailors, in his book *The Voyage `Round the World by Magellan.*

Ferdinand Magellan.

23. GIOVANNI DA VERRAZANO
1485-1528?

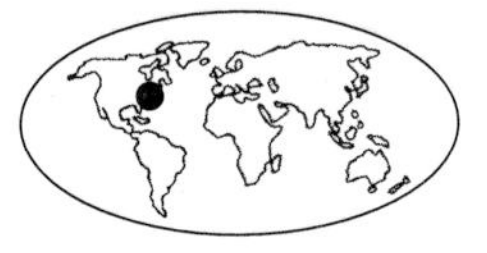

While the Italian city-states did not participate officially in the exploration of North America, many of the sea captains sailing for other countries were Italian. **Christopher Columbus** (see No. 11) was one, and so was **Giovanni da Verrazano**, a native of Florence.

In 1518 Francis I became the first King of France to formally consider the project of colonizing the New World. However, the riches of Asia still beckoned, and Francis joined the ranks of European monarchs who dreamed longingly and greedily of a **Northwest Passage** around the northern edge of North America.

In 1523, a voyage of discovery and exploration was planned with Giovanni Verrazano appointed to head the expedition. It was near the end of the year that Verrazano left Dieppe, on the frigate *Dolphin*, to begin his voyage. He reached the Madeira Islands, where he paused until January of the following year. The weather was unfavorable, the sailing difficult, and it required nine weeks of hard struggle against wind and wave to bring him to the North American coast near present-day Wilmington, Delaware.

Coasting northward, Verrazano discovered both New York and Narragansett bays. At intervals he made landfall and opened a dialogue with the Native Americans, who he reported to be gentle and confiding. Despite this friendly encounter, the Europeans realized that any attempt to colonize the area would put them in conflict with the current residents.

On the coast of Rhode Island, perhaps in the vicinity of Newport, Verrazano anchored for 15 days and there continued his trade with the Indians. Before leaving, however, the French sailors repaid the confidence of the Native Americans by kidnapping a child and attempting to kidnap one of the young women of the tribe.

As Verrazano continued along the coast of New England, he began to find the Native Americans wary and suspicious. They would not buy ornaments, but were eager to purchase iron, knives and other weapons. Verrazano knew that an attempt at colonization here would be problematic.

Verrazano reached Newfoundland in the latter part of May, taking possession in the name of the King of France. On his return to Dieppe, in July of 1524, he wrote a rather rambling account of his discoveries for Francis I. His work, however, was formally recognized by the sovereign, who gave the name New France to that part of the coastline which had been traced by the adventurous crew of the *Dolphin*.

A "French pirate" who was hanged by the Spanish in or about 1527 or 1528 has been identified as being Verrazano.

Giovanni da Verrazano.

24 FRANCISCO DE ORELLANA

1490-1545

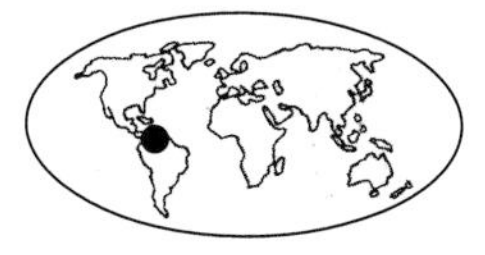

The Spanish explorer of the Amazon, **Francisco de Orellana**, was born in Trujillo. He accompanied his friend **Francisco Pizzaro** (see No. 19) on his voyage to Peru in 1535, and in 1540-1541, he was a lieutenant to Francisco's brother Gonzalo Pizzaro in his expedition in search of Inca treasure that travelled from Quito (in present Ecuador) across the eastern Andes.

In 1541, Pizzaro detailed Francisco de Orellana to travel down the Napo River to get provisions for the rest of the party. For unknown reasons, Orellana and his 60-man crew were sidetracked into the **Amazon River**.

Instead of continuing their assigned mission, they explored the Amazon from its source in the Andes Mountains to the Atlantic coast. After heroic struggles with the climate and with native tribes they reached the Atlantic. They found little of value to take from the Native Americans, but did collect examples of the plant and animal life.

Without returning with Pizzaro's supplies, Orellana returned to Spain in 1542. He brought tales of his exploits on the Earth's widest and second-longest river, and in the world's most vast rain forest. In 1544, Orellana was given control of the government of the territory he had discovered. His later attempts to colonize this vast region failed, and he died of fever, probably in Venezuela.

An account of the Orellana voyage on the Amazon, written for the Spanish king by the friar **Gaspar de Carvajal**, mentioned a race of female warriors the Spaniards had seen. Drawing from folklore, the river was officially named Amazon after the mythological race of women warriors known as Amazons.

Francisco de Orellana.

25. JACQUES CARTIER
1491-1557

Born in St. Malo, France, **Jacques Cartier** earned a reputation as a fearless navigator, and was chosen to head an expedition to America in 1534. It would be France's second major official voyage to America. Two ships were equipped, and after no more than 20 days of sailing under cloudless skies, they dropped anchor on May 10 off the coast of Newfoundland. Like his predecessors, Cartier had hoped and even expected to discover, somewhere in these waters, a passage westward to Asia. While this would never be, he greatly expanded the horizons of what Europeans knew about the geography of North America. By the middle of July, Cartier had circled Newfoundland, crossed the Gulf of St. Lawrence, found the Bay of Chaleurs and had followed the coast as far as Gaspe Bay. It was here that he proclaimed the King of France to be monarch of the land he had surveyed.

Cartier sailed up the **St. Lawrence River**, but decided it to be impracticable to pass the winter in the New World. Cartier turned his prow toward France, and in 30 days he had reached St. Malo in safety. The news of his voyage and its results produced a great deal of excitement.

Jacques Cartier.

Cartier's contribution to exploration was to provide France with enough information about America, to make colonization thinkable. As had been the case in England, the young nobility of France became ambitious to seek their fortune in the New World.

Cartier set out for America again in 1535. Because of heavy seas the coast of Newfoundland was not reached until August. It was the feast day of St. Lawrence, so they gave that name to the river up which they sailed. Making landfall, Cartier climbed to the top of a hill and viewing the scene, he claimed the island for the King of France, and named the town Mont Real (Royal Mountain).

They decided to winter in the New World, but disease and bitter cold took their toll. During the winter, 25 of the French died of scurvy, a mal-

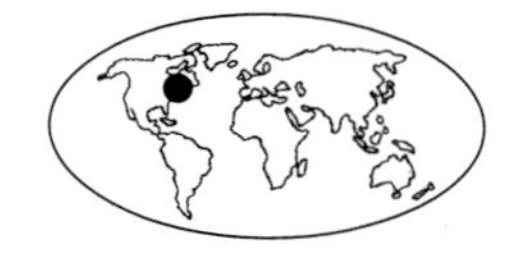

ady hitherto unknown in Europe. Other hardships came with the season. Snows and excessive cold prevailed for months together. Unaccustomed to the rigors of such terrible weather, the French sailors and would-be colonists decided to return to France when spring came. However, before the ships left their anchorage, the chief of the Huron people, who had treated Cartier and his men with great generosity, was enticed aboard and carried off to France, where he would die.

When the fleet reached St. Malo, the accounts which Cartier was able to give of the new country and his experiences caused as much discouragement as his previous voyage had caused excitement. Neither silver nor gold had been found on the banks of the St. Lawrence. The rhetorical question that seemed to be asked was, "What was a New World good for that had not silver and gold?"

In 1541, having been appointed "captain-general" of a new expedition, Cartier was sent on ahead "to the lands of Canada and Hochelaga," which, according to King Francis, "form the extremity of Asia towards the West." His object this time was to found a colony. He established a settlement, which he called Charlesbourg-Royal, on the St. Lawrence at the mouth of the Cap-Rouge. **Jean Francois Roberval**, the newly appointed viceroy, failed to arrive, however, and the settlers became so discouraged and homesick that in the spring of 1542 Cartier took them back to France.

Roberval had originally had difficulty in securing a sufficient number of emigrants. He appealed to the court for aid. The government responded by opening the prisons of the kingdom and giving freedom to whoever would join the expedition. There was a rush of robbers, swindlers and murderers, and the expedition was immediately fully staffed. Only counterfeiters and traitors were denied the privilege of gaining their liberty in the New World.

Five ships under Cartier's command left France — without Roberval, who said he'd come later — in May 1541. They reached the St. Lawrence in good condition and proceeded to the present site of the city of Quebec, where a fort was erected and dubbed Charlesbourg.

Here the colonists spent another difficult winter. Cartier, offended at his subordinate position, was not committed to the success of Roberval's colony, so when the Viceroy and Lieutenant General of New France arrived on a supply ship in June 1542, Cartier secretly got together his own part of the flotilla and returned to Europe. Roberval found himself alone in New France with three shiploads of criminals.

For his explorations Cartier received a patent of nobility, and from 1542 until his death in 1557, he lived comfortably at his home in St. Malo.

Cartier looks at the St. Lawrence from Mont Real.

26. HERNANDO DE SOTO
1496-1542

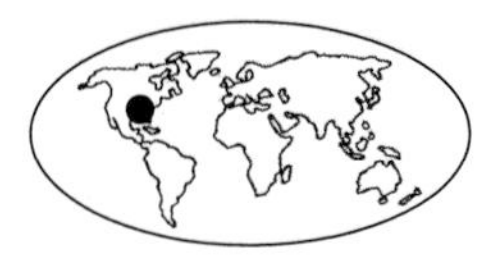

A Spanish soldier and military commander turned explorer, **Hernando De Soto** was born in Badajoz, Estremadura. He served at Darien (Panama) in 1519 and was second in command to Cordova in Nicaragua in 1527, where he was defeated in a feud with Governor Davila. In 1532 De Soto joined the cruel **Francisco Pizzaro** (see No. 19) in his brutal conquest of Peru.

While in Spain in 1536-1537, De Soto was made governor of Cuba, with authority to explore, conquer, and take possession of an ill-defined territory comprising the present Florida.

De Soto set out from Havana in May 1539, landing on the coast of the present Tampa Bay. For three months, the expedition marched into the interior, swimming rivers, wading morasses and fighting Native Americans. October found them on Flint River, where they camped for the winter. In the following spring they set out in a northeasterly direction to find a great city ruled by an empress. The Spaniards reached into what is now South Carolina, and turned westward into the mountains of the present-day states of North Carolina, Tennessee, Northern Georgia and Alabama. They reached the Gulf Coast at Pensacola, where they met supply ships from Cuba.

De Soto then returned to the expedition, and on May 21, 1540, Native American guides brought De Soto to a bluff overlooking the vast river we know today as the Mississippi, and which the Indians called "the Father of Waters." Barges were built, and the Spaniards crossed into what is now Arkansas. They wintered on the Washita River, which they followed upriver to the Red River during the spring of 1541. De Soto's party then returned to the Mississippi and to the Gulf.

In May 1542, after a wide detour that took the group to the mouth of the Red River, De Soto died of fever and was buried. The expedition encountered terrible hardships, many dying from exposure, disease, and Native American attacks. The survivors, about 300 in number, after wandering for a year, reached the Spanish colony at Panuco in September 1543. Like **Christopher Columbus** (see No. 11), De Soto died without realizing the full importance of his discovery.

Hernando de Soto.

27. FRANCISCO DE CORONADO
1510-1554

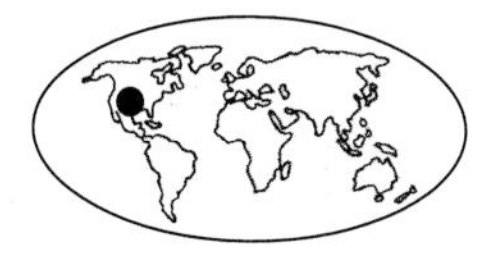

Born in Salamanca, Spain in 1510, **Francisco Vasquez de Coronado** shipped out to Mexico in 1535, and, gaining influence through his marriage with the daughter of a prominent official, was made governor of New Galicia by Viceroy **Antonio Mendoza** in 1539.

In 1540, Coronado became the first European to lead an expedition into the interior of the American West, although other individuals — notably those who brought back the stories of the **Seven Cities of Cibola** and Father de Niza — had been there before.

More important, Coronado was the first to bring *horses* into the American West. These animals were unknown to Native Americans, but as horses were either abandoned by or stolen from the Spaniards, they would quickly be adapted as a vital element in the culture and lifestyle of the Indians of the American West.

Coronado "discovered" the Grand Canyon of the Colorado in northern Arizona and explored the strange and geologically fantastic terrain of the Southwest. He found the Seven Cities, but they turned out not to be solid gold. In fact, they were the great adobe pueblos of the Rio Grande Valley that still exist in the area around present-day Albuquerque and Santa Fe, and which are still inhabited by descendants of the people who lived there when Coronado arrived.

The northernmost of these cities, the Taos Pueblo, is one of the largest, and to this day, one of the best preserved. Another, the "Sky City" at Acoma near Albuquerque, was over 900 years old in Coronado's time and is the oldest continuously-inhabited city in what is now the United States.

Although he had heard about it, Coronado failed to reach the great trading center in the middle of what is now New Mexico, which was later known by the Spanish name **Gran Quivera**. Uninhabited since the late seventeenth century, Gran Quivera was once the key point of contact between the Native Americans of the Southwest and the Plains tribes at the time Coronado visited the region. Coronado did, however, reach the Plains. He got as far north as Nebraska and had contact with the Arapahoe, Caddo, Cheyenne, Comanche, Kiowa and perhaps the Sioux (Dakota) people. Coronado's group were perhaps the first Europeans to see buffalo, which he called "hump-backed cattle."

Coronado returned to Mexico City at the end of 1542, empty-handed and with only half of the troops with whom he had set out. Like the French and English on the Eastern Seaboard, the Spanish did not give up. They came back, established trading posts and missions and eventually found gold, although it was in the mines worked by Native Americans and it was present in smaller quantities than hoped.

Francisco Vasquez de Coronado.

28. SIR MARTIN FROBISHER
1535-1594

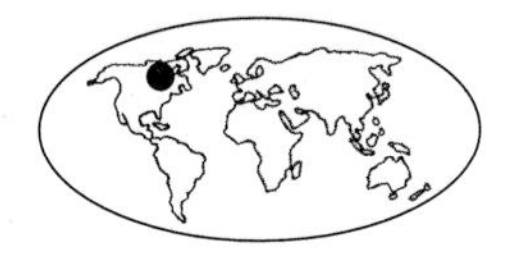

As England turned west across the Atlantic to the promising lands beyond, the spirit of discovery took form under the guiding hand of a bold and skillful sailor, the great sea captain **Sir Martin Frobisher** of Doncaster. Frobisher entered the Royal Navy at the beginning of the golden age of English sea power which came in the 1560s with the reign of **Queen Elizabeth I** (1533-1603), the daughter of Henry VIII and Anne Boleyn.

To understand Frobisher's contributions, one must consider the times. In 1588, the English defeated the Spanish Armada, thus insuring that Britain would be the world's leading maritime power for the next three and a half centuries. With this came the desire to dominate commerce and the urge to explore.

Highly regarded as a navigator, Frobisher received aid from **Dudley, Earl of Warwick**, who fitted out three small vessels and placed them under Frobisher's command. The goal of this expedition was a search of the rumored "Northwest Passage," a sea route around the northern edge of North America to the Pacific and Asia beyond. Three quarters of a century had already been invested in the notion of reaching the rich countries of the East by sailing around America to the north. It was a tantalizing theory, but in fact, the only sea route is perpetually frozen.

Frobisher departed in June 1576. One of his ships was lost on the voyage, and another ship's crew was terrified of the icebergs encountered, and returned to England. Nevertheless, the dauntless Frobisher proceeded to the north and west and discovered the group of islands which lie in the mouth of Hudson Strait.

An inlet on Baffin Island still bears his name. Having visited several Inuit (Eskimo) villages, and having found a piece of gold ore, Frobisher confidently returned to England to happily report that he had discovered the mainland of Asia in what is actually the islands of northern Canada.

England was stirred to action by the excitement surrounding Frobisher's discovery of gold. Elizabeth herself contributed a ship to the new fleet, which departed in May 1577. Frobisher's ships soon came among the icebergs of the far north, and for weeks they were in imminent danger of being crushed in the ice.

The summer was cold and unfavorable. The fleet did not succeed in reaching the same point to which Frobisher had sailed in his single vessel in the previous summer. As the sailors began to grumble, Frobisher decided to return to England. A third fleet of 15 vessels was fitted out, and Queen Elizabeth again contributed personally to the expense of the voyage. In the early spring of 1578 the ships departed for the land of gold. It was the intention to plant there a colony of diggers.

Some were to remain, others to return with the fleet. Twelve ships were expected to come back to England loaded with gold ore. But the third summer was as severe as the others. At the entrance to what was later named as the Hudson Strait, the floating icebergs were so thick that the ships could not be steered among them. The vessels were buffeted about in constant peril of destruction. At last, they made landfall and began taking aboard the mineral resources that were available.

When the fleet returned to England, it was found that the ships' holds contained only dirt and virtually worthless mica — fools' gold! The Northwest Passage was forgotten. The colony which was to be established was abandoned.

Frobisher himself remained in her majesty's navy, but was mortally wounded during an assault on the French port of Brest in 1594.

29. SIR HUMPHRY GILBERT
1539-1583

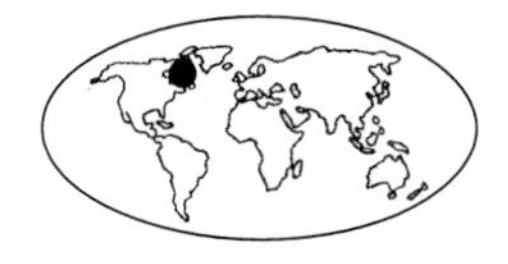

An English seaman, the son of a Devon gentleman, and stepbrother to the illustrious **Sir Walter Raleigh** (see No. 32), **Sir Humphrey Gilbert** was born in Compton. He was educated at Oxford, and served for a short time with the British occupation army in Ireland. Gilbert was among the first Englishmen to conceive a rational plan of colonizing America.

Having written a treatise on the possibility of finding a **Northwest Passage** to India, Gilbert began to consider the more realistic — yet still radical — idea of establishing an agricultural and commercial colony somewhere on the shores of the new continent. If the hope of finding gold had been elusive, he reasoned, certainly the hope of agriculture and commerce would not be.

Sir Humphrey brought his views to the attention of the queen and sought her aid. **Elizabeth I** received his propositions favorably and issued to him a liberal patent authorizing him to take possession of any 600 square miles of territory in America, and to plant there a colony of which he himself should be proprietor and governor.

With this, Sir Humphry, assisted by his stepbrother, Walter Raleigh, prepared a fleet of five vessels, and in June 1583, they sailed for the West. Only two days after their departure, the best vessel in the fleet abandoned the rest and returned to England. Gilbert, however, continued his voyage, and early in August reached Newfoundland. Here he went ashore and took formal possession of the country in the name of Queen Elizabeth.

Events began to get out of hand for Gilbert when some of the sailors discovered a mica deposit in the side of a hill, and it was decided that the mineral was actually silver ore. The crews became excited and began digging the ore and carrying it on board the vessels, while others commandeered two of the five ships to attack Spanish and Portuguese vessels that were fishing nearby.

Sir Humphrey decided to withdraw with three of the ships, but off the coast of Massachusetts the largest of these was wrecked and most of the crew lost. The disaster was so great that Gilbert gave up the expedition and set sail for England. The weather had become stormy and the two ships that remained were unfit.

Sir Humphrey's ship, which was the weaker of the two, was a small frigate called *The Squirrel*. On September 9, 1583, as the storm howled around them and the raging sea rose between them, *The Squirrel* was suddenly engulfed. Not a man of the courageous crew was saved. The other ship finally reached Falmouth in safety.

Sir Humphry Gilbert.

30. SIR FRANCIS DRAKE
1545-1596

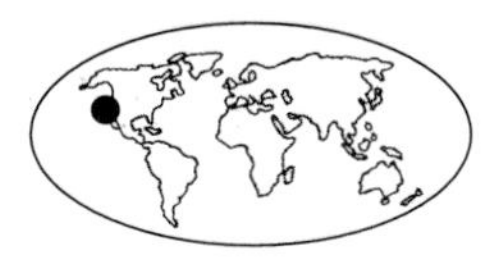

The English naval commander who explored the west coast of North America for **Queen Elizabeth I, Sir Francis Drake**, was born in Crowndale, Devonshire and went to sea at an early age. His ship was one of the two in the West Indies expedition of Jo Hawkins that escaped destruction by the Spaniards in 1567. After two further voyages to the West Indies, he sailed from Plymouth in 1572, successfully attacked the Colombian port of Nombre de Dios on the Caribbean near Panama, and captured several Spanish ships.

Crossing the Isthmus of Panama to the dividing ridge, he became the first Englishman to gaze on the Pacific. In December 1577, Drake sailed with another squadron for the Rio de la Plata, and from there through the Straits of Magellan. Storms left him with only one vessel, the *Golden Hind*, in which he worked his way up the coast of South America robbing Spanish shipping, including the *Cacafuego* with more than £150,000 of treasure. Unable to sail west because of unfavorable winds, Drake went as far north as the present Washington state, and then returned to California. He missed San Francisco Bay because of the fog. A brass plate attributed to Drake was found in 1936 on the shore of San Francisco Bay, but it has since been determined to be a forgery.

Sir Francis Drake.

He landed at what was apparently Drake's Bay near Point Reyes, to repair his ship. Drake was impressed by the area, which he called **New Albion**, because it reminded him of England. Drake stayed for 36 days, explored the country and had himself crowned "King of California" by the Native Americans whom he met.

Drake sailed west to the East Indies, the Cape of Good Hope, and Sierra Leone. He reached Plymouth in September 1580, the first Englishman who had circumnavigated the globe.

In 1585, Drake sailed with a fleet of 25 ships to make reprisals on the Spaniards in the West Indies, and on his return brought back the disheartened colonists from Virginia, and with them, probably for the first time, tobacco and potatoes. In 1587, he destroyed the Spanish shipping in the harbor of Cadiz, and captured a rich port in the East Indies.

When the Spanish Armada appeared the following year, Drake enhanced his great reputation in the running fight up the Channel, and took a leading part in the decisive action off Gravelines.

In 1589, with Norreys, he destroyed shipping at various ports on the Spanish coast. In 1595, he sailed on his last expedition to the West Indies where, after a series of misfortunes, he died at Porto Bello. There is a monument to him at Tavistock, England, and a duplicate in Plymouth.

31. WILLEM BARENTS
1550-1597

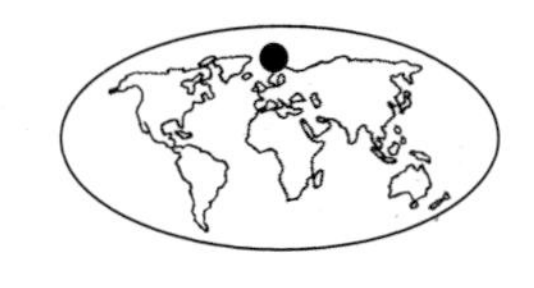

A Dutch explorer, **Willem Barents** was born on the island of Terschelling, and in 1594 he sailed from Holland in search of a Northeast Passage to China. After a month, he sighted and explored the coast of Novaya Zemiya. Barents is today remembered as the namesake of the Barents Sea, part of the Arctic Ocean between Spitsbergen and Novaya Zemiya. The northern part is often filled with ice, but the southern part is usually open to navigation.

He made a second voyage the following year and a third in 1596, during which he discovered the island of Spitsbergen. Sailing eastward, he reached Novaya Zemiya. Having come farther than anyone else in search of the Northeast Passage, he encountered such heavy ice that he and his companions were forced to winter in Ice Haven on the east coast, where they suffered extreme hardships. The following summer, the survivors started for the mainland, but during the voyage, Barents and four of his companions died. In 1871 Captain Carlsen came upon the remains and relics of Barents' winter quarters, which were eventually taken to The Hague.

His explorations and charts would be very important in all the important Arctic voyages for the next 250 years.

Willem Barents, the great Dutch arctic explorer.

32. SIR WALTER RALEIGH
1552-1618

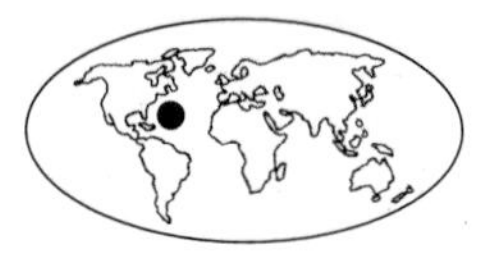

An English courtier, **Sir Walter Raleigh** turned explorer with an eye to establishing an English colony in America. He was born at Haves Barton in Devonshire, and after spending two or three years at Oriel College, Oxford, he became a volunteer in the Huguenot cause in France, and served his apprenticeship as a soldier at Jarnac in 1569. He joined the ill-fated expedition of **Sir Humphrey Gilbert** (see No. 29), his stepbrother, in 1578.

In 1580 he participated in subduing freedom fighters in Ireland, and later served in the Netherlands. During the next few years his expeditions to North America explored the seaboard from Florida to Newfoundland, and in 1585, he established a settlement on Roanoke Island off the Virginia coast. Over the next five years, the colony was left without any communication with England. In 1590, a supply ship found the colony mysteriously deserted, with no evidence of any of the colonists.

Back in England, meanwhile, Raleigh had become a representative of the influence of the Renaissance movement among the upper classes in **Queen Elizabeth I**'s reign. Indeed, his influence at court was often great, and he devoted all his energies to crippling the power of Spain. In 1592 he prepared an expedition, which sailed under **Martin Frobisher**, (see No. 28) but the same year he was imprisoned in the Tower of London as a punishment for a court intrigue.

Having been freed, Raleigh sailed in 1595 to search for gold in Guiana. He sailed up the Orinoco River, but was unable to establish any permanent settlement. In 1596 he took part in an expedition against Spain. Cadiz was attacked and stormed, and a Spanish fleet destroyed. In 1597 Raleigh, along with **Sir Thomas Howard** equipped another fleet to attack Spain, but little was achieved, for the leaders quarreled and stormy weather was encountered. In 1600 Raleigh was made governor of Jersey, succeeding **Sir Anthony Paulet**. He started trade between Jersey and Newfoundland, and did much to promote the island.

With the accession of James I, Raleigh fell into disfavor and was deprived of his office of captain of the guard. His advocacy of war with Spain increased James's disfavor, and in 1603, being suspected of complicity in a plot against the king, he was sent to the Tower of London and tried for high treason. Eventually, James, being in great need of money, released Raleigh to make an expedition to Guiana in quest of gold. Accordingly, on March 19, 1616, Raleigh was allowed to leave the Tower. Though not pardoned, he was full of hope, and started in April 1617. The expedition was a failure, and Raleigh's son was killed. He arrived at Plymouth on June 21, 1618, and was executed on October 29.

Sir Walter Raleigh.

33. HENRY HUDSON
1565-1611

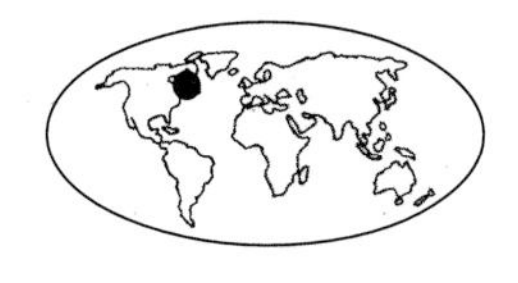

The story of Dutch exploration of North America begins with the illustrious **Henry Hudson**, an English-born Dutch sea captain. On his 1607 voyage, made with a single ship, Hudson had already endeavored to circumnavigate Europe to the northeast. He succeeded in reaching the island of Spitsbergen north of Norway, but was obliged by the rigor of the ice-choked seas to return to England.

With this, the London group declined further support, so the undaunted Hudson turned to the Netherlands. The **Netherlands East India Company**, based in Amsterdam, was actively working toward the goal of exploiting the riches of the East Indies, so Hudson was just the sort of man they were looking for.

They assigned him a small ship called *Half Moon*, and directed him to continue his search for an all-water route to the Indies. It was in July, 1609, when Hudson sailed the *Half Moon* to the shores of Newfoundland.

Henry Hudson.

By September, having sailed as far south as Chesapeake Bay, the *Half Moon* had reached Staten Island and had found a safe anchorage.

In the ensuing days he explored what is now New York Harbor and sailed north on the river to the west of Manhattan island. For eight days, Hudson explored this river which now bears his name. It was a lovely river, but it wasn't the **Northwest Passage**.

On October 4, Hudson sailed for Holland. En route back to Amsterdam, Hudson put in at Dartmouth on the south coast of England, where the ship was detained by orders of King James and the crew claimed as Englishmen. Hudson was obliged to content himself with sending the Netherlands East India Company an account of his great discoveries and his enforced detention in England.

In fact, Hudson was not greatly distressed by his captivity, and as it worked out English merchants furnished the money for another expedition. A ship called *Discovery* was given to Hudson, and in the summer of 1610, he again sailed for the West with a vision of the East Indies on his mind. On August 2, he reached the strait now known as Hudson Strait.

Martin Frobisher (see No. 28) reached this point 32 years before, but no ship had ever before actually entered these waters. However, further to the west the inhospitable shores were seen to narrow again on the more inhospitable sea, and Hudson found himself surrounded with the terrors of winter in the frozen gulf of the north.

In the spring, the crew seized Hudson and his only son, along with seven others who had remained faithful to the commander, threw them into an open boat and cast them off among the icebergs. Their fate remains unknown to this day. The mutineers finally reached England, and were imprisoned.

34. SAMUEL DE CHAMPLAIN
1567-1635

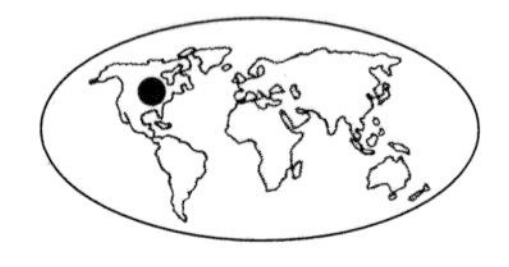

"The Founder of New France," **Samuel de Champlain** was born at Brouage (Saintonge) in France, the son of a captain in the French navy. Having become proficient as a sailor, he served under Henry IV in the war against the Catholic League, and, peace having been declared in 1598, he was made captain of a vessel in a Spanish expedition under **Don Francisco Colombo**, and sent to the West Indies. He also visited Mexico and Panama, where he was impressed with the great value that would accrue to trade through the construction of a ship canal across the Isthmus. He returned to France in 1602 and prepared a report of his journey, first published in English in 1859.

On behalf of **Aymar de Chaster**, Champlain made a voyage to Canada in 1603, proceeding up the St. Lawrence River as far as the site of Montreal.

From 1604 to 1607 he was again in Canada, having sailed with **Pierre De Monts**. They spent one winter on the Isle St. Croix, and then moved to Port Royal . In turn, they explored the New England coast as far south as Buzzard's Bay. Returning to Canada as lieutenant governor in 1608, Champlain founded Quebec, and thereafter spent most of his life in the new French colony appropriately known as New France. In 1609 he discovered Lake Champlain (named in his honor). In his 1613-1615 expeditions, Champlain visited and was the first European to explore (in part) the Ottawa River, Georgian Bay, and the Muskoka Lake region. He later got into a conflict with the Iroquois people that began a traditional warfare between the French (allied with the Hurons) that would continue for more than a century and which would have a great significance in the history of New France.

Samuel de Champlain.

he importance of his discoveries is measured by the fact that he helped extend French sovereignty to large parts of the North American interior.

In 1612 Champlain had been invested with almost vice-regal power in New France, and until his death, with the exception of the period of English possession (1629-32), he was the dominant figure in the colony. Champlain became governor of New France in 1627 under the Company of One Hundred Associates, which the Cardinal founded to help out flagging colonization. When the English captured Quebec in 1628 it was Champlain who succeeded in having the colony returned in 1632.

"In Champlain alone," says Parkman, "was the life of New France. By instinct and temperament he was more impelled to the adventurous foils of exploration than to the duller task of building colonies. The profits of trade had value in his eyes only as a means to these ends, and settlements were important chiefly as a base of discovery."

Champlain kept full journals of his voyages and explorations, and these are of the utmost importance to the study of the history of New France.

35. ETIENNE BRULE
1592-1632

In the early days of American exploration, the Spanish explored and exploited far the interiors of Central and South America as well as the coasts. Meanwhile, the French and English restricted their activities in North America to places that were accessible by boat. Little was known about the interior except for what the French had found on the lower St. Lawrence River. This was, of course, due in large measure to the climate, the hard winters and the icing up of ship channels.

This was the state of affairs in 1608, when **Etienne Brule** came to America. Within the coming years, however, Brule would be the first European to see more of the interior of North America than any Frenchman before him.

Etienne Brule.

Etienne Brule was born in Champigny, France and was a boy when he came to the New World with **Samuel de Champlain** (see No.34). He lived for a year with the Algonquin Native Americans, he learned a great deal about survival in the wilderness, about native languages and about the lay of the land. In 1612, as a member of a party of Huron Native Americans, he visited Georgian Bay and was the first European to see Lake Huron.

He "discovered" Lake Ontario while sailing with Champlain in 1615, and it was on Champlain's instructions that Brule followed the Susquehanna River to its mouth in Chesapeake Bay. Evidence indicates that in 1622, he also may have been the first European to see Lake Superior, the largest body of fresh water on Earth.

In 1629, Etienne Brule is recorded to have turned traitor to the French, and to have sold his services to the British. Legend holds that, three years later, while he was living among the Hurons, he got into a fight with some trappers, and he was killed in a brawl.

36. ABEL JANSZOON TASMAN
1603-1659

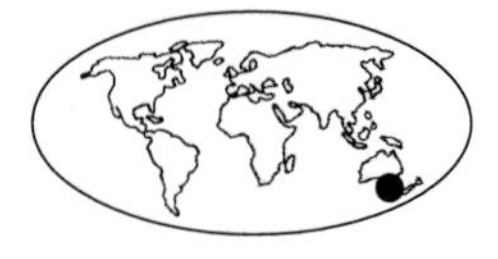

The first great Dutch explorer in the Pacific Ocean, **Abel Janszoon Tasman** was born in Lutgegast. In 1642, while Tasman was in the service of the Dutch East India Company, he was sent out by Van Diemen, governor general of the Dutch East Indies to explore the region around what is now known as Australia. In 1642, he was the first European to visit the island that he dubbed **Van Diemen's Land** after his boss, but which has since been named **Tasmania** after him.

Tasman also "discovered" New Zealand, which he named Staten Land. In 1643, he sailed to Tonga and Fiji, and in the process, he sailed completely around the perimeter of Australia.

He became a commander in 1644, and on a second voyage from the East Indies in 1644-1645, Abel Tasman explored the Gulf of Carpentaria, and the north and west coasts of Australia.

Tasman explored widely and tenaciously. The number of important natural features that today bear his name are testimony to the places he went and the places whose descriptions first reached European notice by way of the journals that he kept. Tasmania is named for him, of course, as well as the **Tasman Glacier** and the **Tasman Sea**. The Tasman Glacier, which he first observed in the seventeenth century, is in New Zealand, in the Southern Alps of South Island, east of the Main Divide, towered over by Mount Cook and the other high peaks. The glacier, said to be the largest outside of the Himalayan and Polar regions, is about 18 miles long and two miles wide. It was discovered in 1862 by Sir Julius von Haast.

The name Tasman Sea was adopted in 1891 by the British admiralty for that part of the Pacific Ocean separating New Zealand from Australia and Tasmania.

Tasman brought home more than notebooks and observations, he brought home a sense of the spirit of adventure that he had tasted in the southwest Pacific. It was this spirit that inspired the Dutch, who were already seafaring people, to go back to the Indies and to build a vast colonial empire that would survive for three centuries.

Abel Janszoon Tasman was the consummate explorer, always searching, always observing and always discovering.

Abel Janszoon Tasman.

37. PIERRE ESPRIT RADISSON
1636?-1710?

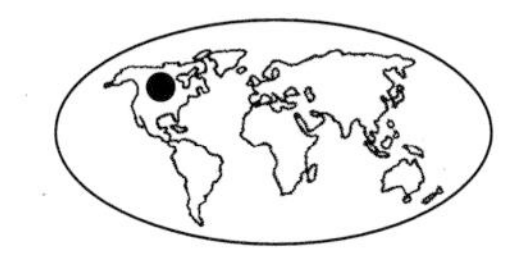

To understand the fire behind exploration, one must understand the economic motivation. For the French in North America it was the fur trade. The French fur trader and explorer, whose reports of fur resources in North America are generally credited with the development of this industry was **Pierre Esprit Radisson**. Along with his brother-in-law, **Menard Chouart des Groseilliers**, Radisson surveyed much of the Great Lakes country in minute detail, which would be useful for scientific as well as economic development.

Each of the European powers viewed the economic development of North America in a different way. The English came primarily to establish a permanent presence on the land itself. The Dutch came as traders. The Spanish came for gold. The French also came for gold, but discovered wealth in furs. While the Spanish searched the Southwest for gold mines, the French explored the **St. Lawrence River** and the Great Lakes country. Beaver were plentiful and the French discovered that their fur was of a high quality. As they exported beaver pelts to Europe, French trappers and traders reached deeper into the heart of what is now the United States than any other nationality.

From the beginning, the French had dominated the lucrative fur trade, but in 1670, England's **King Charles II** (1630-1685) chartered the **Hudson's Bay Company**, which marked the beginning of a major British effort to exploit the resources of the territory north of the St. Lawrence River.

Radisson made four voyages into the interior of the North American continent, on one of which he was captured by the Iroquois but later released at Albany. His last expedition, made with his brother-in-law, took him as far west as what is known now as the state of Minnesota. He returned with a large store of furs which were confiscated by the French in Montreal, who charged him and Groseilliers with trading without a license.

Radisson promptly joined the English and began his long association with the Hudson's Bay Company, which was broken only once, when he rejoined the French to plunder English forts on Hudson Bay. However, he ultimately threw in his lot with the British and later was pensioned by the Hudson's Bay Company.

Pierre Esprit Radisson.

38. JACQUES MARQUETTE
1637-1675

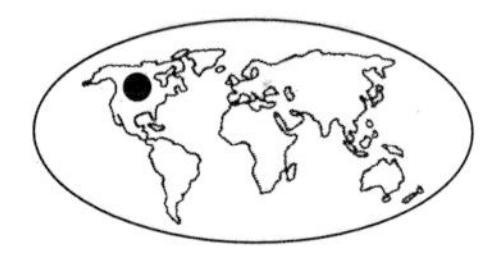

Jacques Marquette was born in Laon, the son of Nicolas Marquette and Rose de la Salle. Jacques entered the Jesuit college in Nancy as a novice in 1654. He became a member of the Society of Jesus, taught in Reims, Charleville, and Langres, and earned a special reputation as a linguist. He was ordered to New France (Canada) as missionary to the Native Americans in 1666, and arrived in Quebec on September 20. His final mastery of six difficult Native American dialects was considered by his colleagues a remarkable achievement.

Jacques Marquette.

In 1668, Marquette left Quebec for Sault Ste. Marie, and in 1669, arrived at La Pointe mission on Chequamegon Bay, Lake Superior, near the present Ashland, Wisconsin. In the spring of 1671, he set up a new mission on the island, but soon moved it to Point St. Ignace, on the mainland four miles northwest. **Louis Joliet**, (see No. 40), dispatched by **Jean Baptiste Talon**, governor of New France, to discover the headwaters of the **Mississippi River** for the French, arrived here in 1672, bearing orders to Marquette from the Jesuit authorities to accompany him. Some men explored for economic gain. Marquette explored to spread a spiritual message.

The expedition, consisting of Joliet, Marquette, and five others, started out in two canoes on May 17, 1673. They crossed Lake Michigan, entered Green Bay and descended the Wisconsin River. They entered the Mississippi on June 17 at Prairie du Chien. After descending the Mississippi to the mouth of the Arkansas, they took the Illinois River, reaching Lake Michigan by way of the Des Plaines and either the Chicago or Calumet River. They went on by canoe, reaching the Jesuit mission at De Pre on Fox River at the end of September.

The following spring, Joliet left for home, but his canoe capsized in Lachine Rapids above Montreal and he lost his maps, diary, and other papers prepared during the winter. Marquette's simple narrative was sent to his superior at Quebec by the hands of Native Americans, and arrived safely. This constitutes almost the entire record of the expedition. Nevertheless, his discoveries about the course of the rivers would aid later expeditions.

The original manuscript journal of this second expedition, continued through April 6, is at St. Mary's College, Montreal.

Owing to illness, it was October 1674 before Marquette could start for the valley of the Illinois to establish the mission he had promised the Native Americans of that region. His goal was to bring Christianity to the Indians, but he also began to lay the groundwork for European settlement of the upper Midwest.

Although successful in his mission, Marquette's illness soon compelled him to attempt the return to St. Ignace, but he died on the site of Ludington, Michigan, on the east shore of Lake Michigan, after much suffering, on May 18, 1675.

39. ROBERT DE LA SALLE
1643-1687

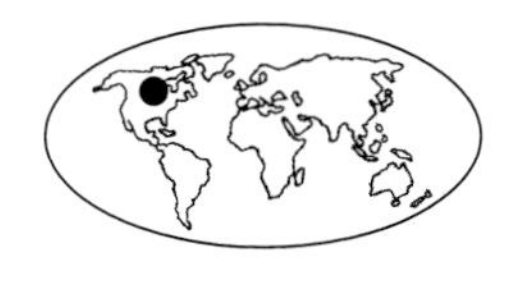

Rene Robert Cavalier Sieur de La Salle was born in Rouen, France and educated by the Jesuits. Compelled by his restless spirit, he came to Montreal in 1666 and took a land grant along the St. Lawrence River. His main interest, however, was in exploring the unknown regions to the west and south and in developing the possibilities of the fur trade with the Native Americans. During the years from 1669 until 1673 he made extensive explorations south of Lake Erie and Lake Ontario, maybe as far as the falls at Louisville.

When **Count de Frontenac** became governor of New France in 1672, La Salle was encouraged to undertake more extensive expeditions. In 1677 he was given a monopoly of the fur trade in the upper Mississippi area and was granted permission to build forts. Two years later La Salle built a small vessel, the *Griffon*, on Lake Erie. In this ship, he sailed to the Green Bay region, where he obtained a cargo of furs to repay his many creditors. The vessel was lost on its return voyage, but La Salle and his party had continued by canoe down the west coast of Lake Michigan to the mouth of the St. Joseph River, where Fort Miami was built (near present-day South Bend).

They went overland to the Kankakee River, and on to Lake Peoria, where a new outpost, Fort Crevecoeur, became a base for the planned exploration of the Mississippi. La Salle then divided his party, leaving his lieutenant, **Henri "Iron Hand" de Tonti**, at the fort, and sending Father Louis Hennepin to explore the upper Mississippi, while he set out for Fort Frontenac to get supplies. Trouble with mutineers and Native Americans forced Tonti was forced to flee.

Undaunted by this series of failures, La Salle and Tonti equipped another expedition which successfully traversed the Illinois country and descended the Mississippi, arriving at its mouth in April 1682.

There he took possession of all the territory drained by the Mississippi, which he named **Louisiana**, for his sovereign Louis XIV. It was a momentous point in North American history, for the Louisiana Territory with its network of trading posts would be the first building block, for good or ill, of European civilization in the Mississippi-Missouri River drainage.

Returning to the Illinois River, La Salle built a new post, Fort St. Louis, on a prominent rock, now known as Starved Rock, where Tonti remained in command. In 1684 La Salle left with an expedition of four ships and 200 colonists to settle at the mouth of the Mississippi.

The expedition missed its destination and landed instead on the present Matagorda Bay, Texas. The colony soon met disaster. After trying unsuccessfully to locate the Mississippi, La Salle set out for Canada, but on the way he was murdered by a mutineer.

Robert Cavalier de La Salle.

40. LOUIS JOLIET
1645-1700

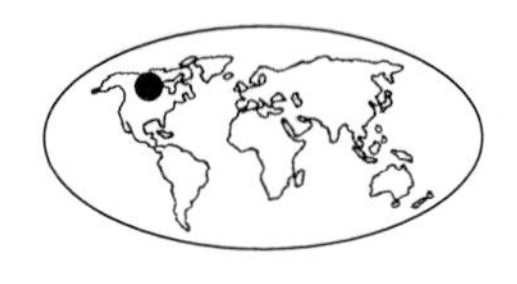

The first of the great French-Canadian explorers actually to have been born in the Western Hemisphere, **Louis Joliet** was born in Quebec in 1645. He was educated by the Jesuits and was destined for the priesthood, receiving the minor orders in 1662. However, he yielded to the lure of the wilderness, and became one of the most adventurous of the early Canadian fur traders and explorers. Ironically, it would be with Father **Jacques Marquette** (see No. 38), a Jesuit missionary, that he would achieve his greatest accomplishments.

Joliet was dispatched by **Jean Baptiste Talon**, governor of New France, to discover the headwaters of the **Mississippi River** for the French, and arrived here at Point St. Ignace on December 8, 1672, bearing orders to Marquette from the Jesuit authorities to accompany him. The lower Mississippi had been discovered by De Soto in 1541 **Pierre Radisson** (see No. 37) may have found its upper reaches in 1655, and La Salle may have been there in 1670, but it is unlikely that either Marquette or Joliet had heard of these claims.

Louis Joliet.

The full historical significance of the expedition as it concerns Joliet, was that for the first time, the French government was undertaking a serious and systematic effort to explore and document the geography of the lasts to the west of the Great Lakes. French trappers had been out there, but no one had undertaken a real survey.

Certainly finding the headwaters of the Mississippi was important, but the key thing was to have a total comprehensive view of the region. This is why Joliet was important. He was an experienced woodsman, but he also understood cartography. Marquette was a vital part of the expedition too, for he was conversant in six native languages. They were a good team.

The expedition, consisting of Joliet, Marquette and a few others, started from St. Ignace in two birch-bark canoes entered the Mississippi on June 17, 1673 at Prairie du Chien. After descending the Mississippi to the mouth of the Arkansas, they knew from reports of Spaniards below that they had in fact found the Mississippi.

In 1674, when Joliet was almost to Montreal, his canoe upset and all of his maps and records were lost.

Joliet went on to visit Hudson Bay in 1679, and received a land grant on the island of Anticosti in 1680, where he engaged in fisheries. He explored the coast of Labrador in 1694, and was, in turn, royal pilot for the St. Lawrence and hydrographer at Quebec.

The importance of Joliet and Marquette's discovery of the Mississippi has been questioned, and it seems possible that Pierre Radisson preceded them, but they were certainly the first to pass down the river for any considerable distance.

41. VITUS BERING
1680-1741

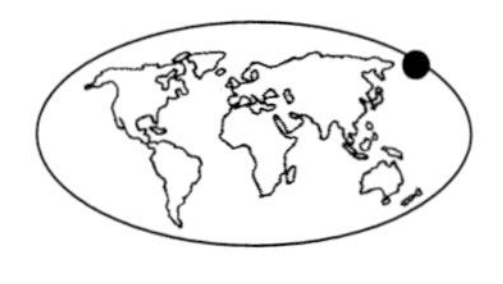

The great Danish arctic explorer **Vitus Jonassen Bering** was born in Horsens, Jutland. His first voyage, made with the Danish navy in 1703, was actually to the sunny climes of the East Indies.

He soon he left the Danish navy and joined the Russian navy in 1704 to fight in the war against Sweden. Bering became an excellent seaman and an officer in the Tsar's navy. He was a natural when it came to seamanship and the naval career fit his interests. After the war, Bering studied navigation and became a trusted part of the Russian naval establishment.

With this in mind, it was small wonder that Russia's Tsar **Peter the Great** appointed him head of a Russian expedition to northeastern Siberia. Setting out from St. Petersburg in 1725, the party proceeded overland to the Kamchatka Peninsula, a difficult trip in itself, especially in the early eighteenth century. From Kamchatka, Bering sailed north in 1728, determined that Asia was not joined to America as was then supposed. In so doing, he succeeded in charting the Siberian shore. He sailed from Okhotsk at the head of a second expedition in 1741, sighted the St. Elias mountain range in Alaska, and reached Kayak Island on the Gulf of Alaska.

On the return voyage, the expedition was forced to land on the island in the Commander Islands group that is now known as **Bering Island**, where he died.

Among the other important geographic features named for Vitus Bering is the **Bering Sea**, the most northerly division of the Pacific Ocean, from which it is separated by the Aleutian Islands.

On the north, the Bering Sea connects with the Arctic Ocean through **Bering Strait**, also named for him.

The Danish explorer who sailed for the Tsar, Vitus Bering.

42. SIEUR DE LA VERENDRYE
1685-1749

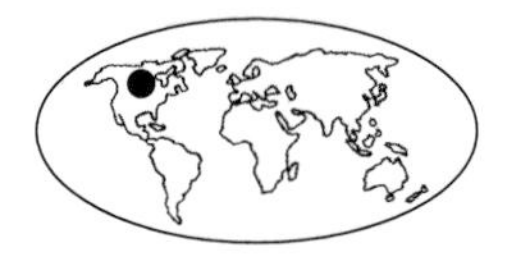

The Canadian-born French explorer, **Pierre Gaultier de Varennes Sieur de La Verendrye** was born in Three Rivers, Quebec. After service with the French colonial army in the French and Native American wars and in Europe in the War of the Spanish Succession (1707-1711), he became a prominent figure in the expansion of New France and the search for the "Western Sea" (the Pacific Ocean).

He obtained a monopoly on the fur trade in the West in 1730, and in the succeeding years, he and his sons made a number of exploratory trips and built posts west of Lake Superior on Rainy Lake, Lake of the Woods, Lake Winnipeg, and the Red and Assiniboine Rivers.

Verendrye went into the West for more than simply an opportunity to get rich in the fur trade. He was intrigued by the vastness of the plains, and the horizon beckoned. In 1738, he reached the Missouri River and travelled through what is now North Dakota. The lure of the horizon was contagious. Verendrye's two sons reached, and wintered in, the Black Hills of present-day South Dakota in 1742-1743. A lead plate which the brothers had buried to claim the upper Missouri Valley for France was found in 1913 near Pierre, South Dakota.

Verendrye and his sons are remembered by the monument in their honor, which is located in west-central North Dakota on the upper Missouri River, about 60 miles southwest of Minot. The monument commemorates the Verendrye explorations in North Dakota in 1738. The monument includes Crow Flies High Butte (named for a Hidatsa Native American chief), on which is a monument to the exploring party.

The prairies and bandlands country as seen by Sieur de La Verendrye.

43. JAMES COOK
1728-1779

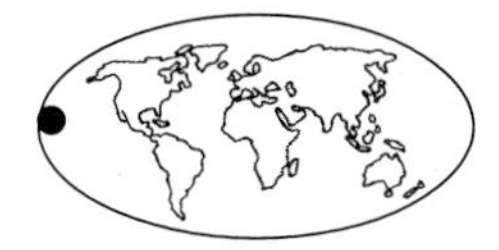

The great explorer of the Pacific, and the first man to sail east around the Earth, **James Cook** was born in Marton, Yorkshire in England. After several years of sailing in the North Sea and Baltic trades, he entered the Royal Navy in 1755, and was assigned to survey the St. Lawrence and the coast of Newfoundland, which he accomplished in 1757.

At the request of the Royal Society, he was sent to the Pacific by the admiralty in 1768 to observe the transit of the planet Venus. He observed the transit from Tahiti, sailed westward, and arrived in England in 1771 after circling the globe the first time. On the way he completed the first circumnavigation of New Zealand by a European and charted its coast. He surveyed the east coast of Australia and sailed through Torres Strait, which separates it from New Guinea, to show that these two lands were not connected.

Captain James Cook.

In 1772, an expedition commanded by Cook was sent out to determine the extent of a reported "southern continent," which was then unconfirmed, and which we now know as **Antarctica**. Cook reached the Antarctic Circle in January 1773, and after skirting the ice in high latitudes, arrived in New Zealand in October.

Cook was an excellent seaman and a tough, no-nonsense British naval officer. He was certainly bitten by the lure of adventure, but he also ran a tight, efficient ship.

He sailed again to the south and east, and in January 1774, reached his most southerly latitude, 71 degrees, 10 minutes. He cruised among the islands of the Pacific during the winter, and set out in the spring to explore the latitudes south of Cape Horn. After discovering South Georgia and sighting Sandwich Land, he sailed for home, reaching England in July, 1775. This voyage, which covered nearly 70,000 miles, was the first circumnavigation of the globe eastward. It also was notable for the dietetic and hygienic measures Cook introduced to successfully prevent any occurrence of scurvy, then a serious menace on long voyages.

Cook, promoted to the rank of captain, received an appointment at Greenwich Hospital. In 1776, he headed an expedition to the Pacific to seek a passage around the north coast of North America. After discovering the **Sandwich Islands** (now known as Hawaii) in 1778. He had come, neither to pillage or colonize, but rather to simply document new lands. However, in Hawaii he was murdered while getting into his boat after trouble with the natives.

The account of the first voyage, written by Cook, is in volumes II and III of *Hawkesworth's Voyages* (1773). That of the second, also written by Cook, was published in two volumes in 1777.

44. GEORGE VANCOUVER
1757-1798

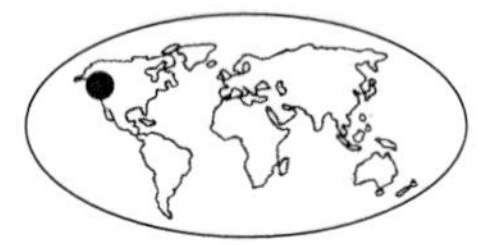

The British navigator who explored much of North America's Pacific Northwest, **George Vancouver** entered the Royal Navy at the age of 13. He became a lieutenant in 1780, after serving on Captain **James Cook**'s second and third voyages of discovery (see No. 43). He was active in the West Indies naval campaigns until 1789, when he was given command of an expedition to the Pacific coast of North America.

Unlike the explorers of the sixteenth and seventeenth centuries, men such as Vancouver and **James Cook** (see No. 43) were not sailing in search of gold and pillage. Nor were they in search of trade routes. Their objective was, at least in part, scientific. Their mandate was to document and map the globe, for Britain envisioned itself to be the world's premier maritime power and to master the oceans, one needed to know them and reveal their mysteries. Of course, along with this was the desire on the part of the King, to have the British flag seen on ships throughout the wold.

George Vancouver.

Vancouver set out in 1791. He sailed around the Cape of Good Hope and surveyed the southwest coast of Australia as well as Dusky Bay, New Zealand.

Reaching the coast of North America, he explored the area from the 35th to the 52nd parallels, or from the present site of the town of Pismo Beach, California to the Queen Charlotte Islands off the coast of present-day British Columbia. In the course of this, he discovered the Gulf of Georgia and in 1793, he circumnavigated what was later named Vancouver Island. Vancouver made two expeditions to the Hawaiian Islands and returned to England, via Cape Horn, in 1795. His travel records, completed after his death by his brother **John Vancouver**, were published in three volumes in 1798 as *A Voyage of Discovery to the North Pacific Ocean and `Round the World in the Years 1790-1795.*

45. WILLIAM CLARK
1770-1838

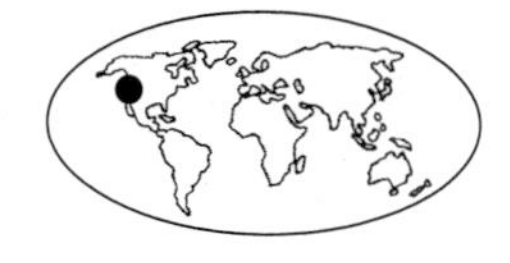

The first great explorer to be born in what is now the United States, **William Clark** was the younger brother of General **George Rogers Clark**, the Revolutionary War hero who secured the western frontier for the United States. Born in Virginia, William entered the US Army under his brother in 1786, served in Native American wars, and resigned with the rank of lieutenant in 1796. He re-entered the army as a second lieutenant in 1804, and, with **Meriwether Lewis** (see No. 47), led the historic expedition of the **Louisiana Purchase**.

The two names of Lewis and Clark are inextricably linked in our historical memory because of the unprecedented two-year expedition which they undertook that succeeded in surveying more of the North American continent than any previous expedition. It gave the United States its first sense of its geographic importance.

In 1803, President **Thomas Jefferson** concluded an agreement with **Napoleon Bonaparte** to purchase a vast tract of North American territory owned by France and named for King Louis XIV. Lewis and Clark assembled a group of surveyors, scientists and others and sailed north from St. Louis, Missouri, on the Mississippi River, on March 14, 1804. During the spring and summer of 1805, Lewis and Clark split up and between them explored much of what is now the state of Montana.

They joined up again on August 17 and crossed the **Continental Divide** in the Rocky Mountains, and with the help of the Shoshone, Nez Perce and Flathead Indian tribes, they travelled to the Clearwater River, where they constructed long boats for a trip down the Snake River and ultimately into the great Columbia River.

On November 7, the expedition reached the mouth of the Columbia at the Pacific Ocean. They finally returned to St. Louis in September 1806.

Their scientific and ethnographic report to Washington was a milestone in the documentation of North America's natural history. It was their providing this detailed, scientific data about Louisiana that bore the true importance of what they had done. Thanks to their efforts, the people of the United States, still a new country, could now conceive of being part of a nation that stretched from ocean to ocean.

In 1807, Clark was promoted from first lieutenant to brigadier general and superintendent of Native American affairs of the Louisiana Territory. He served as governor of Missouri Territory from 1813 to 1821; as surveyor-general of Illinois, Missouri, and Arkansas (1825); and as federal superintendent of Native American affairs from 1822 to 1833.

William Clark.

46. DAVID THOMPSON
1770-1857

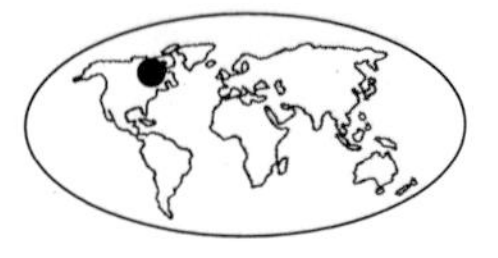

The great Canadian explorer **David Thompson** was born in London, England and started working for the **Hudson's Bay Company** at the age of 14. He remained with them until 1797, when he joined the **North West Company**.

During his career, David Thompson undertook numerous exploring trips, both for the companies with which he was connected and for the British government. In 1807 he crossed the Rocky Mountains by way of the Howse Pass. In 1811 he ascended the Columbia River by canoe from the Canoe River to its source.

Thompson was the member of a generation of explorers, which included the American "mountain men" such as **Jim Bridger** (see No. 56), who went into the frontier areas to seek their fortune not through plunder, but simply through getting an ordinary job that would allow them to work in an environment that they loved. The two companies for whom Thomson worked represented the British commercial effort to obtain the valuable pelts of North America's noble beaver. The French explorers had discovered the value of the fur trade, but in England was anxious for its share. With this in mind, King Charles II chartered the Hudson's Bay Company, which marked the beginning of a major British effort to exploit the resources of the territory north of the St. Lawrence River. The North West Company was a later rival. These companies needed men like David Thompson.

The wealth of detail in Thompson's map of western Canada, which he finished after he left the Northwest in 1812, was to prove invaluable to later expeditions. From 1816 to 1826 he surveyed the boundary between Canada and the United States.

David Thompson.

47. MERIWETHER LEWIS
1774-1809

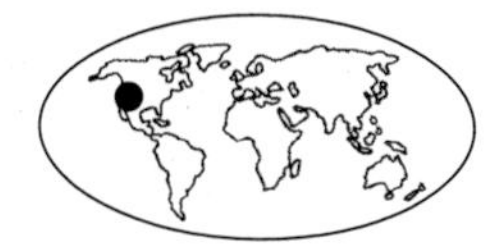

Born near Charlottesville, Virginia, **Meriwether Lewis** enlisted in the US Army in 1795, and he served with **William Clark** (see No. 45) at the close of the Native American wars in the Northwest Territory, where he excelled in his ability to command troops in the wilderness.

In 1801, during his first term of office, President **Thomas Jefferson** chose Lewis as his private secretary. Jefferson was aware of Lewis' military record and respected him as a disciplined officer. In 1803, Jefferson chose him to lead the expedition to explore the newly-acquired **Louisiana Purchase** and to discover a land route to the Pacific Ocean.

Lewis chose **William Clark** (see No. 45) as a co-commander of the expedition. The Louisiana Purchase had nearly doubled the size of the United States, but it was an immense, mysterious place that few men had ever seen. They assembled a group of surveyors, scientists and others and sailed north from St. Louis, Missouri, on the Mississippi River on March 14, 1804.

Meriwether Lewis.

During the spring and summer of 1805, Lewis and Clark split up and between them explored much of what is now the state of Montana. They joined up again on August 17 and crossed the **Continental Divide** in the Rocky Mountains, and with the help of the Shoshone, Nez Perce and Flathead Indian tribes, they travelled to the Clearwater River, where they constructed long boats for a trip down the Snake River, and ultimately into the great Columbia River.

On November 7, the expedition reached the mouth of the Columbia at the Pacific Ocean. Three months later, they began the difficult journey back up a network of rivers to the Divide. Again, the two men travelled separate routes, meeting at the headwaters of the Missouri River on August 11, 1806. On September 23, they returned to St. Louis. Lewis and Clark brought back a thorough documentation of the vast region that Jefferson had added to the new nation.

Appointed governor of the Louisiana Territory in 1807, Lewis proved to be an excellent administrator. However, on a trip to Washington, he died mysteriously in central Tennessee. While some believe he took his own life, he was probably murdered.

48. SIR JOHN ROSS
1777-1856

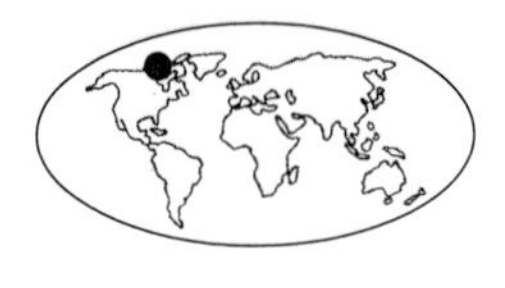

The legendary British admiral and Arctic explorer **Sir John Ross** was born at Balsarroch in Wigtownshire and began his career of Arctic discovery in 1818 with a voyage to Baffin Bay. Also destined to be a great chronicler of exploration, he published his book *Voyage of Discovery* in 1819.

An important goal of exploration for the three centuries preceding Ross's time had been the searches for the rumored "**Northwest Passage**," a sea route around the northern edge of North America to the Pacific and Asia beyond. **Martin Frobisher** (see No. 28) of Doncaster, with aid from Dudley, Earl of Warwick, tried to find it in 1576, as had Henry Hudson and many others. Three centuries had already been invested in the notion of reaching the rich countries of the East by sailing around America to the north, when, from 1829 to 1833, Ross was employed on another Arctic expedition.

Ross was troubled by his failure to find the Northwest Passage, but as a naval officer, he did what he was ordered. His *Narrative of a Second Voyage in Search of a Northwest Passage*, published in 1835, told the disappointing tale.

Though Ross did not realize it, the Northwest Passage was little more than a tantalizing theory. In fact, the only sea route is the perpetually-frozen Arctic Ocean that was not practically navigable until the use of icebreakers and nuclear submarines made it more routine in the latter twentieth century.

Sir John Ross.

In 1850, Ross led an expedition to the Arctic in search of **Sir John Franklin** (see No. 50), who had set out in 1845 in an attempt to discover the Northwest Passage and was last seen in July of that year.The relief expeditions discovered that Franklin's party had wintered at Beechey Island, but had perished in 1846 near King William's Land.

Sir John Ross was also the author of *A Treatise on Navigation By Steam* (1828), *Memoirs of Admiral Lord de Saumarez* (1838), and *On Intemperance in the Royal Navy* (1852). In his books, Ross left the legacy of practical knowledge of what he had learned commanding ships in difficult arctic seas.

49. ZEBULON PIKE
1779-1813

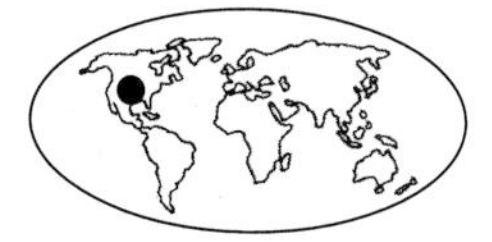

The American soldier and western explorer **Zebulon Montgomery Pike** was born in Lamberton, New Jersey. In 1799 he was commissioned in the US Army, and he became a brigadier general on March 12, 1813. Just as the British Royal Navy was an instrument of national policy in its mapping of the world's oceans, so too was the US Army an instrument of national policy in the mapping of the North American continent.

With his aptitude for navigation, Pike was to become part of this effort. In 1805 he was ordered to find the true source of the Mississippi River. Showing great energy and perseverance, Pike became the army's favored choice to do exploration work.

In 1806 he was sent to explore the headwaters of the Arkansas and Red rivers, leaving St. Louis on July 15. From the Osage towns on the Missouri River, he struck across the prairie in a southwesterly direction, finally reaching the Arkansas, ascending that river to the Rocky Mountains in what is now Colorado. It was here that he discovered the prominent peak that bears his name. Pike's Peak rises abruptly at the edge of the Great Plains at the southern part of the Front Range of the Rockies. Pike discovered it in 1806, but did not, as some suppose, actually climb it. The peak was first ascended in 1820 by the scientist Dr. **Edwin James** and a party of explorers.

The documentation that Pike compiled on his expeditions was to prove valuable for future generations of explorers and settlers coming into Colorado. During the Colorado gold rush of 1859, Pike's Peak was an important landmark for the prospectors.

Zebulon Montgomery Pike.

Turning south in search of the Red River, Zebulon Pike was arrested by Spanish authorities at Santa Fe and sent to Chihuahua, but finally was allowed to return to the United States, through Texas. He reached the Louisiana frontier on July 1, 1807.

On the outbreak of war with England in 1812, Pike was assigned to the Northern Department under General Henry Dearborn (1751-1829). Pike commanded the brigade which captured York (Toronto) on April 27,1813, but he was killed by the explosion of a powder magazine.

50. SIR JOHN FRANKLIN
1786-1847

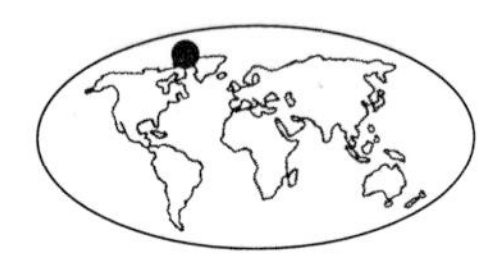

The British Arctic explorer who was the namesake of one of Canada's vast Northern Territories, **Sir John Franklin** was born in Spilsby, England. He joined the Royal Navy in 1800, serving until 1818, when he commanded the *Trent* in an unsuccessful expedition to cross the Polar Sea.

In the early nineteenth century, as Franklin was beginning his career England was growing in its importance as the world's leading sea power, and in he would devote his career and eventually give his life to advancing this ideal. In order to be a major maritime power, England needed to be first in charting the world's oceans and in knowing the best trade routes. One of the most elusive of the latter was the **Northwest Passage** and it was in search of this route that Franklin sailed in 1819.

He explored the northern coast of the American continent from the mouth of the Coppermine River eastward. He went up the coast to Point Turnagain, and returned across the badlands. He led a second expedition in 1825-1827, which descended the Mackenzie River to the Arctic, and then went west to Return Reef where he turned back. This effort permitted the mapping of a long stretch of the coast.

In May 1845, with two ships, he embarked from England in an attempt to discover the Northwest Passage and was last seen in July 1845. It was not until 1848 that a series of relief expeditions were sent out to find what had happened. They discovered that Franklin's party ascended what is now known as Wellington Channel, wintering at Beechey Island. They were stopped by ice near King William's Land, where they spent the winter and where Franklin died.

It was established in 1859 that Franklin had achieved his goal, the discovery of the Northwest Passage, but he probably didn't realize it, and if he had, he would have been the first to confirm that it was virtually useless because of the ice. Franklin was posthumously promoted to a rear admiral five years after his death.

Sir John Franklin.

51. JEDEDIAH STRONG SMITH
1799-1831

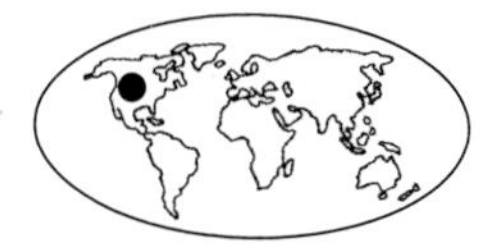

A legendary American fur trader and explorer, **Jedediah Smith** was born in Bainbridge, New York. Like the Canadian explorer **David Thompson** (see No. 46), Smith got his first taste of the West through the fur trade. In 1822, having gone west to Illinois. In 1822, he became one of William H. Ashley's Rocky Mountain trappers. In 1824 Smith and Thomas Fitzpatrick led a trapping party into Wyoming, through South Pass to the Green River Valley.

On this trip, Smith fell in love with the West and decided to devote himself to travelling its trails and exploring its mysteries.

Another important result of the trip was that Smith surveyed and identified what was to become the crossing point on the Continental Divide that would be used by the **Oregon Trail**.

In 1826 Smith, along with **David E. Jackson** and **William L. Sublette**, purchased Ashley's interests in the Far West, and continued the business until 1830.

Jedediah Strong Smith.

The explorations for which Smith became famous were carried on between 1826 and 1828 in the Great Basin, that vast, largely unknown area between the Great Salt Lake, the California deserts, the Pacific Ocean, and the Columbia River. With a party of 15, Smith set out from the Great Salt Lake to discover an overland route to California.

With two men, Smith proceeded east across the interior deserts to the Great Salt Lake. Ten days later, with 19 men, he again started for California over his previous route. While crossing the Colorado River, nine trappers were killed by Mohave Native Americans. The survivors reached the California mission settlements and again went north to the Stanislaus River base camp.

After being detained by the Mexican authorities in California, the entire party started north through the Siskiyou wilderness for the Willamette Valley and the Columbia River. At the Umpqua River in Oregon all but Smith and two others were killed by Native Americans. The survivors made their way to Fort Vancouver, from which they journeyed up the Columbia River to the rendezvous in Idaho.

Smith retired from the fur trade in 1830, and in 1831, with Jackson and Sublette, he entered the St. Louis-Santa Fe trade on the Santa Fe Trail. It was at a Cimarron Desert water hole in Kansas that he was murdered by Comanche Native Americans. Smith was the first white American to extensively examine the Great Basin of the West, to reach California by an overland route, and to travel overland from California to the Columbia River.

His explorations had great influence upon the ultimate official attitude toward the Far West (that it was integral to the United States) and stimulated the popular principle of "Manifest Destiny."

52. CHARLES WILKES
1798-1877

An American naval officer and explorer, **Charles Wilkes** was born in New York City. Entering the US Navy after a few years' service with the merchant marine, he was appointed to head the Depot of Charts and Instruments in 1833.

In 1838-1842 he commanded the first United States expedition to Antarctica, which came to be known as the Wilkes Expedition. During the voyage, Wilkes and his crew surveyed the Antarctic continent, as well as about 280 Pacific islands, and the Pacific coast of North America. It was an expedition that charted more land and sea territory than any previous attempt to explore the Antarctic and the Pacific, with the possible exception of that of **James Cook** (see No. 43).

Captain Charles Wilkes.

Wilkes was a contemporary of the British Antarctic explorer **James Clark Ross** (see No.55), and the two men have natural features in Antarctica named for them. The Ross Ice Shelf is adjacent to the vast plain known as Wilkes Land.

A captain at the beginning of the Civil War, Wilkes was in command of the USS *San Jacinto* when, on November 8, 1861, it intercepted the British mail steamer *Trent* in the Bahama channel. Aboard, he found and captured James Mason and John Slidell, the Confederate commissioners to Britain. The *Trent* Affair, as it was known, was a diplomatic powder keg.

The USS *San Jacinto* seizing the *Trent*.

At first, Wilkes was applauded, but the Lincoln administration grew nervous over the possibility of Britain becoming allied with the Confederacy and declaring war on the United States, so the prisoners were released. In 1866, Charles Wilkes retired as a rear admiral, having played a role in the establishment of the US Naval Observatory in Washington. He died on February 8, 1877.

53.54. FREDERIC CAILLIAUD and RENE CAILLIE 1787-1869, 1799-1838

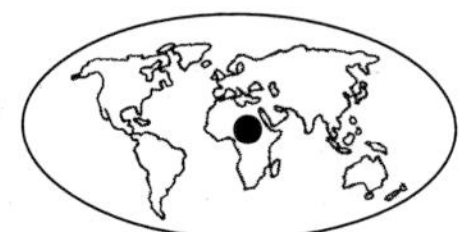

Frederic Cailliaud and **Rene Auguste Caillie** were a pair of French explorers who were extremely important in the process of surveying the geography of North Africa. The effort would lead to France's vast colonial empire in the region. Their importance is measured both in their survey work and in the fact that they did it on behalf of France and they were in the forefront of establishing a French presence in Africa.

Cailliaud was born at Nantes in 1878 and was involved in the expedition to Egypt in 1815. During this, he succeeded in locating the ancient emerald mines of Jebel Zubara, and made other important archaeological discoveries in the oases of Siwah.

Rene Auguste Caillie (or Caille) was born at Mauz in Poitou. In order to operate in North Africa, Caillie learned Arabic, studied Islam and wore native attire.

In 1828, he became the first European to make the long trip to the ancient and fabled trading center at Timbuktu (Tombouctou), deep in the heart of the Sahara in what is now Mali. As the first European to make this journey safely, he was awarded a prize from the Geographical Society of Paris.

Rene Auguste Caillie.

Frederic Cailliaud and friends racing camels.

55. SIR JAMES CLARK ROSS
1800-1862

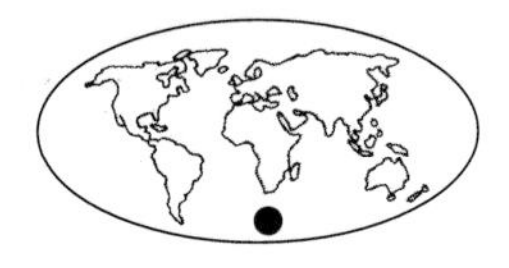

The nephew of British explorer **Sir John Ross** (see No. 48), **Sir James Clark Ross** is perhaps better known than his uncle, and was certainly more successful and far-reaching in his expeditions. Sir James made Arctic expeditions with **Sir W. E. Parry** in 1819-1827, and with his uncle in 1818 and 1829-1833.

Sir James Ross established the location of the north magnetic pole in 1831 and assisted with a magnetic survey of Great Britain in 1838.

During explorations in the Antarctic area between 1839 and 1843, Ross, now an admiral, discovered what are now known as the Ross Sea and Ross Island and Victoria Land, which he named for the queen. Ross reached the 78th parallel, the farthest south that would be reached by *anyone* for 60 years. In 1848-1849 Ross commanded the *Enterprise* in an expedition searching for **Sir John Franklin** (see No. 50). Sir James Ross later wrote *A Voyage of Discovery and Research to Southern Antarctic Regions*, which was published in 1847.

Ross' importance as an explorer lay in the fact that he was the first to begin a systematic examination of Antarctica's natural features. Others had been to Antarctica, but Ross examined it. While this would not provide Britain with any direct economic benefit, because colonization is impractical and mining too difficult, it did advance pure scientific knowledge. In the nineteenth century, when Britain imagined itself to be the world's only true global superpower, the idea of being in the forefront of obtaining scientific knowledge about the world's distant regions was vital.

Among his most lasting monuments are Antarctica's Ross Sea and the massive Ross Shelf Ice, which rises from that sea.

Sir James Ross set a record for southern exploration which stood for 60 years.

56. JIM BRIDGER
1804-1881

An American fur trader, explorer, and scout, **James "Jim" Bridger** was born in Richmond, Virginia. In 1812 moved with his family to an Illinois farm across the Mississippi from St. Louis, Missouri. In 1822 he joined William H. Ashley's trapping expedition to the Rocky Mountains, which also involved **Jedediah Smith** (see No. 51).

Like Smith, Bridger was important in the history of exploration because he devoted himself to a thorough exploration of the West. Others before them had pioneered direct routes *through* the West, but Smith and Bridger devoted their efforts to exploring the area in a detailed way.

For 20 years Jim Bridger trapped and explored the vast country from the Missouri River to western Utah, and from the headwaters of the Columbia to New Mexico. The history of every state in the Rockies has a chapter devoted to him.

During his day, he knew more about the terrain of the vast and rugged West than any other non-native man alive. Expeditions sought his assistance as a guide, for his knowledge of the lay of the land was both legendary and encyclopedic.

It is believed that in 1824 Jim Bridger was the first white man to visit the Great Salt Lake. By 1842 he had established the trading camp which later became the noted Fort Bridger on the Oregon Trail in Uinta County, Wyoming.

During the years from 1849 to 1867, Bridger knowledge and reliability led to his being repeatedly employed as a guide or scout for government military and scientific expeditions and private parties in the Far West. In 1868, after nearly half a centurty in the mountains, he retired to his farm near Kansas City, Missouri, where he died in 1881.

Mountain man Jim Bridger.

Jim Bridger knew Wyoming's Green River area well.

57. JEAN LOUIS AGASSIZ
1807-1873

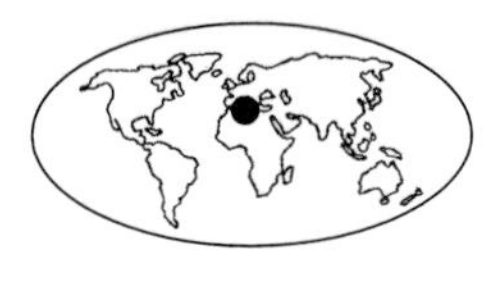

In the early years of exploration, the explorers were motivated by an urge to see new places and penetrate the unknown, and they were bankrolled by commercial interests who saw the potential for economic gain. By the nineteenth century, a new generation of explorer began to emerge. These were the explorers who explored for sake of scientific discovery, where economic interests were secondary or non-existent. The first of this new breed were the geographers (such as the Antarctic explorers), who came to explore the lay of the land. Next came the biologists who and geologists, who came to document the nature of the new environments. Foremost among these was **Jean Louis Rodolphe Agassiz**.

He was born in Switzerland and educated at the universities of Zurich, Heidelberg, Erlangen, and Munich. He devoted much time to the study of natural history, and prior to his graduation prepared a description of the fishes of Brazil (from specimens gathered under the patronage of the king of Bavaria), which elicited a warm response from the French naturalist Baron **George Leopold Cuvier** (1769-1832), with whom he was later closely associated.

In 1832 Agassiz became professor of natural history at the University of Neuchatel, and in 1833, he began to publish his *Researches on the Fossil Fishes*, which the following year brought him the Wollaston Prize in London. This work, comprising five volumes of text and five of plates appeared at intervals from 1833 to 1843. In 1839 he issued the first part of his *Histoire Naturelle des Poissons d'eau Douce de l'Europe Centrale*, which was completed in 1842. His work on the fossil echinoderms of Switzerland appeared in 1839 and 1840, and from 1840 to 1845 he published *Etudes Critiques sur les Mollusques Fossiles.*

In 1836 Agassiz began an examination of glacial phenomena. He made some of the earliest recorded observations on the motion of glaciers, and embodied his scientific observations in *Etudes sur les Glaciers* (1840) and *Nouvelle Etudes* (1847). His theory of glacier motion (dilation of water frozen in the crevasses) soon gave way, however, to that formulated by Stephen Forbes (gravitation plus plasticity).

In October 1846, Agassiz visited America, and delivered a course of lectures on *The Plan of the Creation*. These established his reputation, and during the winters of 1847 and 1848 he lectured in the principal cities of the United States, everywhere with success. In 1848 he was elected to the newly founded chair of natural history in the Lawrence Scientific School at Harvard University, and in the summer of that year, in company with a class of students, he made a scientific expedition to the northern shores of Lake Superior.

At the invitation of Professor Louis Bache, superintendent of the US Coast Survey, he spent the winter of 1850-1851 in an expedition to the Florida Reefs, his report upon which was afterward published in the Memoirs of the Museum of Comparative Zoology. In 1851, in addition to his work at Cambridge, he accepted a professorship at the Medical College of Charleston, SC, and delivered a series of lectures at the Smithsonian Institution.

In 1865, he embarked on an important scientific expedition to the Amazon, in which he studied the natural history and published his *A Journey to Brazil.* He was accompanied by his wife, **Elizabeth Cabot Cary Agassiz** (1822-1907), the American educator and author of *A First Lesson in Natural History* (1859) and *Seaside Studies in Natural History* (with her son, 1865). Agassiz is memorialized by mountains in Utah and Switzerland, and a glacier in Glacier National Park, Montana, which are named for him.

58. DAVID LIVINGSTONE
1813-1873

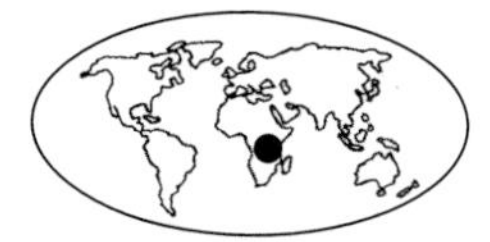

David Livingstone was Scottish missionary whose name heads the pantheon of nineteenth century African explorers. In 1840, he received the diploma of the Glasgow Faculty of Physicians and Surgeons. In the same year he was ordained a missionary by the London Missionary Society and set sail for the Cape of Good Hope, settling in Bechuanaland in what is now South Africa.

He was fascinated with Africa nd yearned to learn the secrets of the place that Europeans described as "The Dark Continent." In 1849 Livingstone set his missionary work aside and began his explorations with a journey to Lake Ngami and the Zambezi River, which he surveyed. Again, in 1852, he reached the Zambezi at Sesheke, ascended the river, crossed the watershed to the Kasai region, and reached the coast at Luanda. Retracing his steps to Sesheke, he passed down the river and became the first European to see Victoria Falls.

David Livingstone.

Visiting England, he related the data from his travels, much of which was being heard in England for the first time. He became a celebrity and various honors were conferred upon him Returning to Africa, Livingstone returned to the Zambezi region, having severed his connection with the London Missionary Society, and accepted the post of consul at Quelimane in 1858. From 1858 to 1864, with Dr. (later Sir) **John Kirk**, he explored the Zambezi and Rovuma rivers, and "discovered" Lake Nyasa in 1859. Returning to England in 1864, Livingstone spent about a year at home and paid a visit to India before starting on his last journey into Africa.

His great object now was to discover the ultimate sources of the Nile. In April 1866, he landed at Mikindani, from where he hiked along the Rovuma River and the southern end of Lake Nyasa, and across the Luangwa and Chambezi rivers to the southern end of Lake Tanganyika, or, as he called it, Liemba. He travelled to the shore of Lake Mweru, and then visited the chief Kazembe near Lake Bangweulu in 1869. He crossed Lake Tanganyika, and came to Ujiji where he would live for the next two years, cut off from all communication with the outside world. Though suffering severely from illness, he made a difficult expedition to the Lualaba at Nyangwe.

His illness had become severe and debilitating by the time that he was reached at Ujiji in October 1871 by **Henry Morton Stanley** (see No. 64), who had been sent out by the *New York Herald* to find him. Stanley returned to the coast, taking with him Livingstone's journals, while he hiked southward in 1872. They proved to be an invaluable geographic record.

Skirting the southeastern shore of Tanganyika, Livingstone struggled on until he reached Chitambo village, south of Lake Bangweulu, where he died. His body was carried by his faithful followers to the coast, and was buried in Westminster Abbey.

59. JOHN CHARLES FREMONT
1813-1890

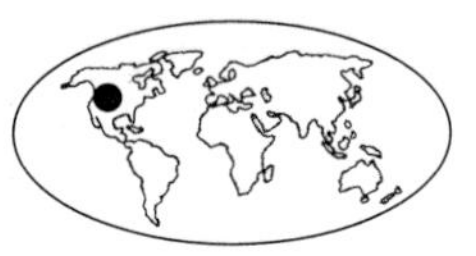

The American explorer, soldier, and later politician **John Charles Fremont** was born in Savannah, Georgia. After serving briefly as a math and engineering teacher in the US Navy, he accepted a job as a civil engineer in the US Army. In 1838 he was commissioned as a second lieutenant of topographical engineers.

Fremont gained early fame for his western explorations. In 1842 he made an expedition to southern Wyoming, and in 1844 he went to the mouth of the Columbia River, and south to the Sacramento Valley. His reports on California and the Great Salt Lake region turned American attention toward both areas at a time when "Manifest Destiny" (America's natural right to own the land in the West) was the guiding policy in the direction of national expansion. His third expedition, in 1845-1847, took him to California, in whose "conquest" he unquestionably wished to have a part. By February 1846, he had posted his US Army troops at San Jose, in the heart of California.

John Charles Fremont.

Fremont in the Rockies in 1842.

The Mexican authorities ordered him to leave the country, but he refused, playing for time. He knew that war between the United States and Mexico was expected. He was one of a growing number of Americans who felt that California should be part of the United States and he was intent on doing his part to facilitate this.

At Sutter's Fort near Sacramento, he encouraged the discontented American settlers in the Sacramento Valley to revolt. It should be pointed out that there were, at this time, more American settlers than Mexican nationals, living in California. News of the outbreak of war reached him in July 1846, and from then on he actively supported Commanders Robert Stockton and John Sloat in the military conquest of California.

At the close of the war in 1848, Stockton commissioned him civil governor of California, but Fremont was soon ousted in the bitter quarrel between Stockton and General **Philip Kearny** over lines of authority in the new territory. Nevertheless, his dream of an American California was a reality.

As a result, Fremont was court-martialed and dismissed from the service, but President James Knox Polk remitted the sentence, allowing him to resign.

60. ROBERT O'HARA BURKE
1820-1861

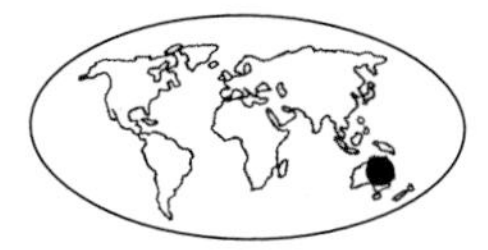

Even today, the Great Australian Desert is a formidable place. Comprising 1.5 million square miles, it is the second largest desert on Earth after the Sahara. The first European, and possibly the first person of any nationality, to lead an expedition across it from south to north was **Robert O'Hara Burke**.

Born in Galway, Ireland, he was one of those nineteenth century idealists who believed that humans had the power to triumph over nature's harshest environments. In August 1860 (late winter in the Southern Hemisphere), Burke led his expedition out of Melbourne. Disagreements and infighting occurred some weeks out, and at Cooper's Creek some members of the party turned back. Burke continued on, and reached the mouth of the Flinders River on the Gulf of Carpentaria. Although he starved to death on his return, Burke had achieved his goal.

Robert O'Hara Burke.

The Australian outback, where Burke perished.

61. SIR RICHARD BURTON
1821-1890

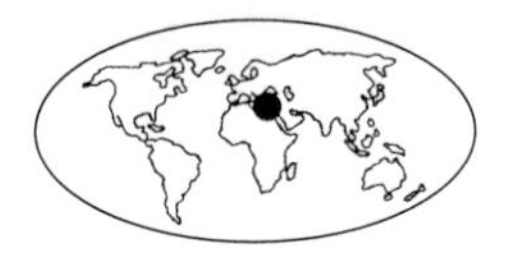

Born in Hertfordshire, England, **Sir Richard Burton** was a noted British traveller, linguist, and author whose writings informed the West about important regions of the world in the nineteenth century. Entering the East India service in 1842, he explored the Nilgiri Hills, served for five years in Sindh, and in 1851 published *The Unhappy Valley,* supplemented by a volume describing the people inhabiting the valley of the Indus River.

Having returned to England, Burton set out for Arabia in 1853, and "assuming the character of a wandering dervish," he succeeded in reaching the holy shrines of Mecca and Medina. The account of his adventures, entitled *Narrative of a Pilgrimage to El Medina and Mecca,* appeared in 1855-1856. In 1856 he accompanied an expedition to the lake region of Central Africa, which resulted his being one of the first Europeans to see Lake Tanganyika and the Victoria Nyaza. The expedition was reported in his *Lake Regions of Equatorial Africa* (1860).

Because of his difficult temperament and his impatience with protocol and official procedure, Burton was constantly at odds with the Foreign Office and never attained the rank which his services merited.

He did serve as British consul at several important overseas locations which were described in the lexicon of the time as "exotic" because of their remoteness and their having robust, non-European cultures. Among these were Fernando Po, Santos in Brazil and and Damascus.

As a prolific writer, his greatest literary achievement was probably his *Thousand Nights and a Night* (1885-1888), an erratic but lively translation of *The Arabian Nights*.

The importance of his work both as an explorer and as a writer was in his astute documentation of the lifestyle and folklore of the people in the regions he visited.

In his later travels he was accompanied by his wife, Isabel, who tried without much success to correct Burton's unsocial tendencies. After his death she destroyed several of his manuscripts which she considered pornographic, notably his translation of "The Scented Garden," an erotic Arabic work.

Sir Richard Francis Burton.

62. FERDINAND HAYDEN
1829-1887

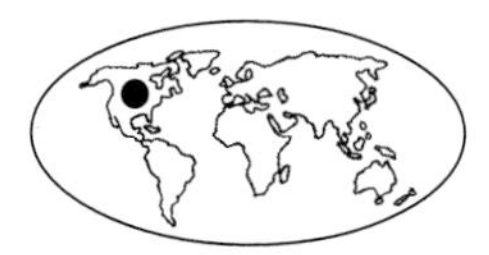

An American geologist born in Westfield, Massachusetts, **Ferdinand Vandeveer Hayden** did more to systematically and scientifically survey the western United States than anyone before him. The creation of Yellowstone National Park as the first national park in the United Stares is one of his crowning achievements and one of his most enduring legacies.

Ferdinand Vandeveer Hayden.

As a geologist, his motivation was purely scientific. Having studied at Oberlin College, Hayden spent most of the years from 1853 to 1879 exploring in the Rocky Mountains, the Black Hills and the Great Basin, although he took time off during the Civil War to serve as a surgeon in the Union Army. From 1865 through 1872 Hayden was professor of geology at the University of Pennsylvania, but he spent his summers on horseback in the West. Hayden headed Division One of the US Geological & Geographical Survey of the Territories, while **John Wesley Powell** (see No. 63) headed Division Two.

In 1871, Hayden's team, which included the legendary location photographer **William Henry Jackson** (1843-1942), began a systematic survey of the Yellowstone country, scientifically recording and photographing its amazing features for the first time. In March 1872, thanks to Hayden's report and Jackson's photographs, **Yellowstone National Park** came into being.

Hayden's expeditions also reached the headquarters of the Yellowstone, Madison, and Gallatin rivers in Montana and explored much of the Colorado Rockies, beginning in 1873. Hayden was largely responsible for the setting aside of the area now known as **Rocky Mountain National Park.** As a scientist, he wanted to see natural features preserved.

When the former US Geological & Geographical Survey of the Territories became the US Geological Survey, Hayden remained part of the new organization until 1886. He edited the first eight reports of surveys made in Nebraska and other territories between 1867 and 1876. He has had a fossil and 44 genera and species named for him.

63. JOHN WESLEY POWELL
1834-1902

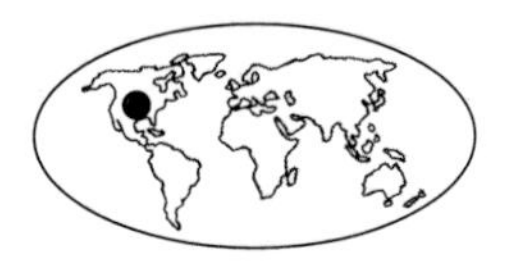

The great American geologist and western explorer **John Wesley Powell** was born in Mount Morris, New York. He studied at Oberlin and Wheaton colleges, and served during the Civil War with the Union forces, rising to the rank of major of artillery. He lost his right arm during the Battle of Shiloh, but accomplished a great deal in his later life, despite this disability.

After the Civil War, Powell was a professor of geology at the Illinois Wesleyan College from 1865 to 1868. As such, he was one of the first to conduct parties of students to the West.

In 1869 he secured financial assistance from Congress and the Smithsonian Institution to explore the Colorado River, particularly the **Grand Canyon of the Colorado**, and made the first successful boat trip down that river for nearly 900 miles. Among those on his expedition team was **John K. "Jolly Jack" Hillers**, one of the first and most important photographers to document the West.

In John Powell's report, *Explorations of the Colorado River of the West and Its Tributaries* (1875), revised as *Canyons of the Colorado* (1895), he made the now-accepted assertion that the canyon had resulted from the cutting action of the river upon rocks that were being gradually elevated.

Part of the US Geological & Geographical Survey of the Territories, Powell's team, including Hillers, returned to the West each year between 1871 and 1873. Powell was especially interested in documenting these areas scientifically. Working mainly from March through September, they conducted further surveys of the Grand Canyon, as well as the Parunuweep, Virgin and Zion canyon country.

In 1879, John Wesley Powell was appointed as director of the US Bureau of Ethnology. When the various Western survey groups (including his own Division Two of the US Geological & Geographical Survey of the Territories) were merged as the US Geological Survey, he served as its director from 1880 to 1894.

Major John Wesley Powell.

64. HENRY MORTON STANLEY
1841-1904

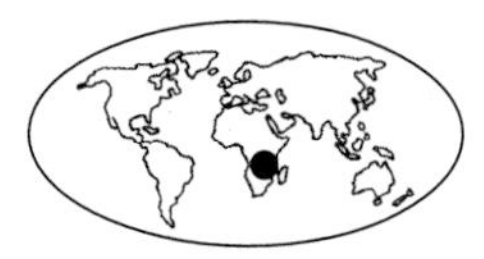

Claimed by the British who were enthralled by his accomplishments, **John Rowlands** was actually born in Wales, and moved to the United States in 1859. He took the name of his first employer there, becoming **Henry Morton Stanley**.

He served in the army of the Confederacy from 1861 to 1862, and the US Navy from 1863 to 1867, becoming an American citizen in 1862. He accompanied the British army to Ethiopia in 1868 as a correspondent for the *New York Herald*, and in 1869 was commissioned by James Gordon Bennett of the *Herald* to find the British missionary **David Livingstone** (see No. 58), who was thought to be lost in the African interior. Setting out from Zanzibar in March 1871, he found Livingstone at Ujiji in November, and in the next year joined him in exploring Lake Tanganyika. He returned to Europe with Livingstone's journals and papers, and received Queen Victoria's thanks.

Henry Morton Stanley.

After covering the Ashanti expedition in 1873 for the *Herald*, Stanley made a second extensive journey into the African jungles, during which he circumnavigated Lake Victoria and Lake Tanganyika, and followed the Lualaba River from Nyangwe to the west coast, proving it identical with the Congo (Zaire) River.

Fascinated with Africa, Stanley turned from reporting to exploration himself. Between 1879 and 1884 he was again in the Congo region, assisting the International Congo Association in setting up the Congo Free State, under Belgian auspices. On his last important African trek in 1887-1889, he travelled from Zanzibar to Lake Albert to rescue Emin Pasha. On the way, he documented the Ruwenzori Mountains and Lake Albert Edward. Stanley resumed his British citizenship in 1891, sat in the British Parliament from 1895 to 1900, and was knighted in 1899.

Stanley wrote a number of popular accounts of his adventures, including *How I Found Livingstone* (1872), *Through the Dark Continent* (1878), *In Darkest Africa* (1890) and *Through South Africa* (1898). The theme of his books was to convey the wonder he had experienced in Africa.

65. ROBERT EDWIN PEARY
1856-1920

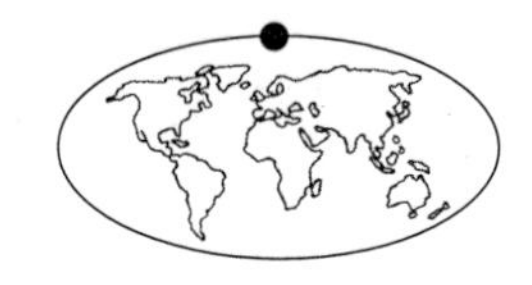

The American Arctic explorer **Robert Edwin Peary** was the first human being to stand at the **North Pole**. Born in Cresson, Pennsylvania, he worked for the US Coast & Geodetic Survey as a surveyor and draftsman, and then joined the US Navy as a civil engineer in 1881. In this role, he took part in surveys for the proposed Nicaragua Canal between 1884 and 1887.

Peary visited Greenland for the first time in the summer of 1886, when he travelled 50 miles into the interior from Disco Bay on reconnaissance. On a second expedition in 1891-1892, he spent 13 months in north Greenland, making a 1,200-mile sled journey to Independence Fjord in the northeast and determining that Greenland is an island. He also began ethnological studies of the "Arctic Highlander" Inuit (Eskimo) people of Greenland. In 1893-1895, he repeated the trip to Independence Fjord, and discovered the great meteorites of Cape York, which he secured on summer voyages in 1896 and 1897.

Peary's next voyage lasted four years (1898-1902). He crossed to Ellesmere Island in 1899 and connected his surveys of west Greenland with those of **James Booth Lockwood** (1852-1884) in Grant Land in 1883. In 1900 Peary journeyed from Lady Franklin Bay and rounded the northern extreme of Greenland. In 1902, proceeding from Cape Hecla in north Grant Land, he started for the North Pole, but the condition of the ice forced him back.

With new equipment and the ship *Roosevelt* designed for Arctic conditions, another voyage was launched in 1905. This time Peary's party, heading north from Grant Land, reached the 87th parallel, the "farthest north" of any non-Inuit explorer to that date, 200 miles from the North Pole. But again ice conditions forced him back. The expedition was recorded in Peary's book *Nearest the Pole* (1907).

The final expedition (1908-1809), again in the *Roosevelt*, reached Cape Sheridan in August, and established winter quarters there. They set out on March 1, 1909. Peary, along with **Matthew Henson** (1866-1955) and four Inuits, sighted the Pole on April 6 and explored it for 30 hours.

Peary received the thanks of Congress by special act in 1911, and retired from the Navy with the rank of rear admiral. He received honors from the National Geographic Society, the Royal Geographical Society, and the French Legion of Honor. In 1913 he was a delegate and secretary to the **International Polar Commission**. He wrote *Northward over the Great Ice* (1898), *The North Pole* (1910), describing his last Arctic expedition, and *Secrets of Polar Travel* (1917).

Robert Edwin Peary.

66. FRIDTJOF NANSEN
1861-1930

The Norwegian explorer and statesman **Fridtjof Nansen** was born in Store Froen and educated at the University of Christiania. He visited the east coast of Greenland in 1882 to acquire zoological specimens, and became curator of the Natural History Museum in Bergen. After crossing the ice fields of Greenland on skis in 1888, he described his achievement in *The First Crossing of Greenland* (1890). Heading a North Polar expedition in 1893, he sailed on the *Fram* to the New Siberian Islands, and from there, the ship drifted north in an ice floe for two years. In 1895, Nansen, accompanied by **F.H. Johansen**, left the ship and set out by dog sled for the Pole. They reached a point 184 miles farther north than any previous explorer had been, and where they spent the winter in Franz Josef Land. They returned to Norway with the Jackson-Harmsworth expedition.

Fridtjof Nansen.

Nansen, prominent in the movement for the peaceful separation of Norway from Sweden, became the first Norwegian minister to England in 1906. He resigned to become a professor of oceanography at Christiania University, and made several cruises to the North Atlantic before World War I.

He was chairman of the Norwegian Association for the League of Nations (1918), and later a delegate to the League Assembly. Requested by the first council of the League to investigate the prisoner of war problem (1920), he returned 450,000 prisoners to their homes, and supervised League relief work among Russian, Greek, and Armenian refugees. A special identity certificate was devised to serve as an international passport for refugees; this was known as a "League of Nations" or "Nansen" passport. For directing Red Cross famine relief work in the Volga Valley and southern Ukraine region (1921-1923), Nansen received the Nobel Peace Prize in 1922.

He represented Norway on the League Disbarment Committee (1927), and prior to his death, was planning a dirigible trip to the North Pole.

In addition to several volumes on his explorations, he wrote *Norway and the Union with Sweden* (1905), *Russia and Peace* (1924) and *Armenia and the Near East* (1928).

67. ELIZABETH COCHRANE
1867-1922

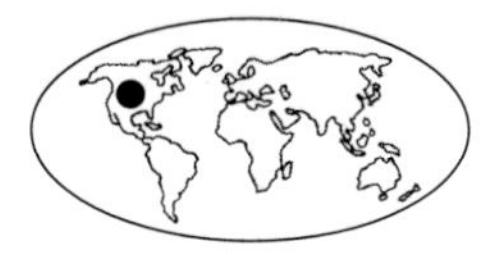

While most explorers included in this book set out to distant reaches of the Earth and beyond in order to investigate a place, Elizabeth Cochran set out to distant reaches of the Earth to investigate time.

Born in a small town in Pennsylvania, **Elizabeth Cochrane** grew up in Pittsburgh. Shunning marriage, she searched for a job but her delicate appearance made her unfit for even kitchen work. A scathing letter in support of women's rights to the Pittsburgh *Dispatch* earned the 18-year-old a $5-a-week position there. Cochran chose **Nellie Bly**, the title of a popular song, for her pen name.

Elizabeth "Nellie Bly" Cochrane.

As Nellie Bly, she penned opinionated articles for the series "Our Working Girls," and factories began banning reporters from their premises. Undaunted, she got a job making copper cables and shocked Pittsburgh with vivid descriptions of the horrible working environment. This clandestine approach became Bly's much-imitated trademark. In 1887, she moved to New York City, and again couldn't find a job. Finally, the *World* offered her a trial assignment: fake insanity in order to investigate an insane asylum. Her widely read reports on its cruel, unethical staff and inhumane conditions brought changes to the institution.

In November 1889, with much fanfare, she accepted the challenge of beating the fictional record of Jules Verne's *Around the World in 80 Days* (1873), and Bly set out to circle the globe in 80 days or less. It was a day and age when women didn't do things like that and she earned a great deal of admiration. She travelled at a breakneck pace by steamship, train, rickshaw and sampan. In San Francisco, when the passengers on her ship faced a two-week quarantine because their health reports had been left in Japan, "Nellie" threatened to swim to shore, and a tugboat transported her to a waiting train. Seventy-two days, six hours and 11 minutes after she left, she enjoyed a hero's welcome in Jersey City, New Jersey.

Bly wrote a best-selling account of her trip and maintained a column at the *World*. Covering the bloody Pullman Strike outside Chicago, she was one of the few journalists to sympathize with the workers. In 1895, Bly married a wealthy industrialist, Robert Seaman. After his death, she took over his business, providing employees with health care and equal wages. A string of misfortunes left the company bankrupt, and Bly went to Austria for a much-needed rest. When World War I broke out, leaving her stranded abroad, the New York *Evening Journal* hired her as a correspondent, making her the first woman to cover the battlefront. Once back in the United States, Nellie Bly continued exposing corruption and aiding the oppressed.

68. ROBERT FALCON SCOTT
1868-1912

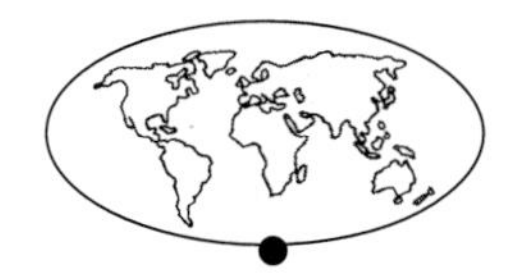

Born in Devonport, England, **Robert Falcon Scott** entered the Royal Navy and served as commander of the research vessel *Discovery* in 1900. He headed the National Antarctic Expedition to the South Pole. Scott discovered King Edward VII Land and reached the 52nd parallel, the farthest south at that time. Scott wrote *Voyage of the Discovery* (1905).

He returned to Britain in 1904 and was promoted to captain. In 1910 Scott left on a second expedition to the Antarctic, sailing in the *Terra Nova.* The objective of the mission was to be the first expedition to reach the **South Pole**. The American **Robert Peary** (see No. 65) had been the first to reach the North Pole in 1909, and the British were anxious to see the Union Jack as the first flag to fly at the South Pole. It was a race to the Pole that was very similar to the race for the moon undertaken by the Americans and the Soviet Union in the 1960s. As with the moon race, the Polar competition stretched the technology to the limit, but Scott was well supported with all the best, and he was confident, even though the Norwegians, under **Roald Amundsen** (see No. 70) were also on the ice at the same time. What a bitter disappointment it must have been when Scott and his party reached the South Pole on January 18, 1912, only to find Amundsen had already been there. Delayed by bad weather, Scott and his companions ran out of food before they could make it back to their base camp. Tragically, they perished from starvation and exposure. Later the same year a search party found the bodies of the men and the records and Scott's diary, containing a full account of the tragic expedition.

Robert Falcon Scott.

The terrain faced by Scott ranged from difficult to impossible.

69. NILS OTTO NORDENSKJOLD
1869-1928

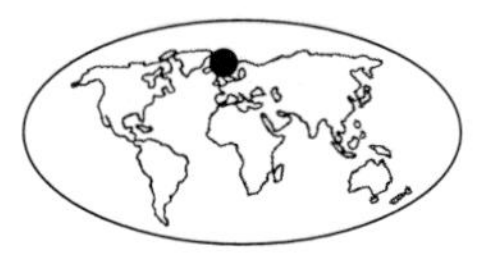

The great Swedish geologist and explorer **Nils Otto Gustaf Nordenskjold** (1869-1928) was born in Sjogelo, Smaland in Sweden. Nordenskjold attended the University of Uppsala, taught at the University of Goteborg, and took part in scientific expeditions to Tierra del Fuego and Chile in 1895-1897, to Alaska in 1898, and to Greenland in 1900.

He led a Swedish scientific expedition to Louis Philippe Land in the Antarctic in 1901, and was rescued by an Argentine expedition in 1903 after his vessel had been crushed by ice. He conducted a geographical survey of the of the Amazon headwaters in the Andes in 1905, returned to Greenland in 1909, and explored the Andes in Chile and Peru in 1920-1921.

Nils Otto's uncle was also an important Arctic explorer. **Nils Adolf Erik Nordenskjold** (1832-1901) was born in Helsingfors (Helsinki) in Finland, and educated in geology at the University of Helsingfors. He left Finland because of political difficulties, and after 1857 made Sweden his adopted country.

He served as the staff geologist on several expeditions to Spitsbergen, the remote island (claimed by Norway) that exists far to the north of Scandinavia. Nordenskjold became the director of the Royal National Museum in Stockholm in 1858, and led an Arctic expedition in 1868 which reached the 81st north latitude.

After voyages to the Yenisei River in Siberia during 1875 and 1876, in 1878, Captain Nordenskjold, now Baron Nils Nordenskjold, sailed from Sweden (1878) to seek a Northeast Passage. He completed his circumnavigation of Eurasia in 1880. He had little influence on the places he visited, but the maps he made were useful for future navigation in the Arctic regions.

The Baron later visited Greenland in 1883 and Spitsbergen again in 1890.

Nils Otto Nordenskjold.

An Arctic fjord.

70. ROALD AMUNDSEN
1872-1928

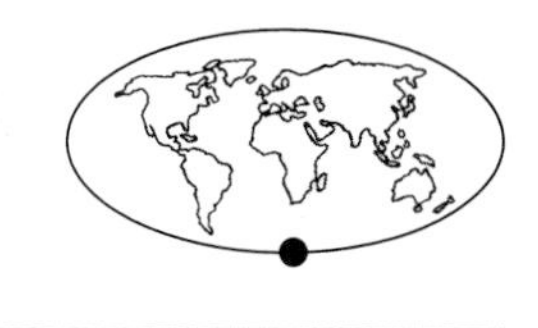

The Norwegian Arctic and Antarctic explorer who was the first man to reach the **South Pole**, **Roald Amundsen** was born in Borge. Educated at the University of Christiania (now Oslo), he left the study of medicine to take up a more exciting career as an Arctic explorer. Entering the Norwegian Navy, he later became first officer on the *Belgica*, of the Belgian South Polar Expedition of 1897-1899.

On his return, he planned an expedition to locate the North Magnetic Pole and to discover the **Northwest Passage**. Sailing in 1903 aboard the *Gida*, he succeeded in relocating the position of the North Magnetic Pole, proving that it probably is in continual movement and has no fixed position. By taking teams of hunters as well as dog sleds, Amundsen was able to live off the land as his ship worked its way through the Arctic. His was the first expedition to actually sail through the Northwest Passage, reaching Herschel Island in 1905.

By this time, the dangerous race was on to be the first to cross the forbidding Antarctic continent and reach the South Pole. Several expeditions were vying for the honor, and Amundsen's was one of them. Sailing in the *Fram* in 1910, he established a base on the Great Ice Barrier in the Bay of Whales. By dog sled, he reached the South Pole on December 16, 1911, a few weeks ahead of Captain **Robert Scott** (see No. 68), who would die tragically after reaching the Pole.

In the ship named *Maud Amundsen*, Amundsen successfully negotiated the Northeast Passage in 1918-1920. After failing to reach the North Pole by airplane with Lincoln Ellsworth in 1925, Amundsen, Ellsworth, and **Umberto Nobile** (see No. 73) flew over the Pole in 1926 in the *Norge*, a semi-rigid airship in June 1928. Amundsen was died in 1928 during a failed attempt to rescue rescue Nobile's expedition which had become lost in the Arctic.

He was the first man to see both poles and to traverse both the Northwest and the Northeast passages. He wrote *My Life as an Explorer* (1927) and *Our Polar Flight* (1925, with Ellsworth) and *First Crossing of the Polar Sea* (1927).

Roald Amundsen.

71. CHARLES WILLIAM BEEBE
1877-1962

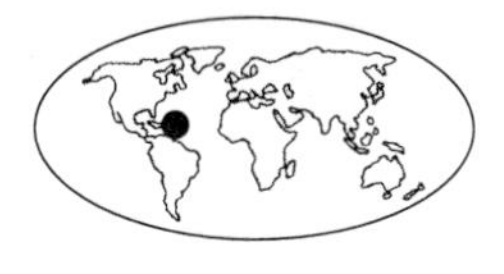

While the period 1492 through the nineteenth century was noted for famous, as well as infamous, explorations of the surface of the Earth, the twentieth century would be noted for exploration beyond the surface of the Earth. This would include both voyages into space and voyages beneath the surface of the Earth's oceans.

One of the first to explore the more remote depths of the oceans was the American naturalist **Charles William Beebe**. Noted for his work in marine biology and ornithology, Beebe was born in Brooklyn, New York and studied at Columbia University.

In 1899, he became curator of ornithology for the New York Zoological Society. and during the next decade developed its collection of living birds into one of the foremost in the world. On his appointment as director of the society's department of scientific research in 1916, Beebe established a station in the Bartica jungle of British Guiana and devoted himself to adding to the existing knowledge of birds and other animals of the tropics. He later led scientific expeditions to Asia, Africa, and South America.

Beginning in 1930 he used an airtight spherical chamber known as a bathysphere, nicknamed a "diving bell" to take himself to incredible depths. He used the bathysphere extensively in studying the deep sea life off Bermuda. It was on August 15, 1934 that Beebe, along with bathysphere designer **Otis Barton**, reached a depth of 3,028 feet. No human being in a bathysphere or submarine would surpass this record for a quarter of a century.

Beebe also employed the *Arcturus* in exploring the Sargasso Sea in 1925. He observed the marine life of the eastern Pacific from the glass-bottomed *Zaca* in 1938. Beebe was the author of many scientific volumes which were as noted for their literary charm as for their authenticity. These included *Two Bird Lovers in Mexico* (1905), *Edge of the Jungle* (1921), *Galapagos: World's End* (1923), *Jungle Days* (1925), *Beneath Tropic Seas* (1929), *Half Mile Down* (1934), *Book of Bays* (1942) and *High Jungle* (1949).

Charles William Beebe.

72. ROY CHAPMAN ANDREWS
1884-1960

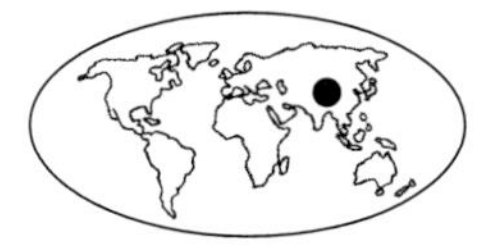

One of the twentieth century's most remarkable naturalist explorers, **Roy Chapman Andrews** was born in Beloit, Wisconsin, and graduated from Beloit College in 1906. He went to work for the American Museum of Natural History in New York and first specialized in whales, leading and going on expeditions to study and collect them. These field excursions took him to the seas off Vancouver Island and Alaska in 1908, the Dutch East Indies in 1909-1910, and Korea and Japan in 1911-1912.

Roy Chapman Andrews.

During World War I, he served in Naval Intelligence in China and Mongolia, and this experience gave him the idea for postwar activities that would make his mark on the history of archeology and paleontology.

After exploratory expeditions into Central Asia from 1916 to 1919, he led expeditions there which proved of great historical and archaeological interest. He revolutionized exploration in the region by shunning bactrian camels in favor of automobiles. The cars needed more fuel than the camels, but they could cover much greater distances and areas.

For its day, Andrews' automobile expedition was a revolutionary innovation. The Andrews expedition discovered geological strata previously unknown and extensive evidences of primitive life in the central Asian Plateau, including the first dinosaur eggs ever found. The dinosaur finds alone were a milestone in the history of paleontology.

Andrews retired from active work with the Museum of Natural History in 1942 to serve as director. He wrote such popular but scientifically accurate accounts of his expeditions as *Whale Hunting with Gun and Camera* (1916), *On the Trail of Ancient Man* (1926), *The New Conquest of Central Asia* (1932), and two autobiographical books, *Under a Lucky Star* (1943) and *An Explorer Comes Home* (1947). Other fiction and non-fiction accounts of places he had explored included *Meet Your Ancestors* (1945), *Quest in the Desert* (1950) and *Heart of Asia* (1951).

73. UMBERTO NOBILE
1885-1978

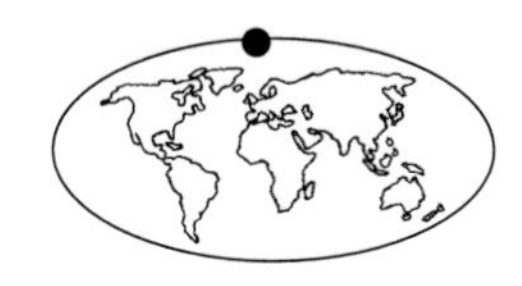

The Italian engineer and explorer **Umberto Nobile** both designed and built the semi-rigid airship *Norge*, which carried the Amundsen-Ellsworth Expedition in the first-ever flight over the **North Pole** in 1926. With Nobile as pilot, the *Norge* flew from Rome to the North Pole and on to Teller, Alaska. This great exploit was followed by a newspaper quarrel between Nobile and the other two leaders as to the share of credit for the success.

Two years later, Nobile, having decided to fit out an all-Italian Arctic expedition, built a larger airship, called *Italia*.

Setting out with 15 others, Nobile flew over the North Pole, but on May 28, 1928, they ran into high head winds while trying to return to King's Bay. Ice jammed the *Italia*'s controls and it went down. The control car broke off with ten men aboard. The remainder of the airship blew away with the remainder of the crew, who were never seen again.

A huge international rescue effort found the survivors on June 28, and they were rescued by a Soviet icebreaker. However, five people, including Arctic explorer **Roald Amundsen** (see No. 70), lost their lives in the rescue effort and Nobile was blamed because the failure of the *Italia* had precipitated the disaster. However, in January, 1931, Nobile was awarded a gold medal by the US Congress for polar exploration.

In the 1930s, Nobile drifted away from exploration to pursue his interest in aviation. Nobile left Italy for the Soviet Union and conducted research on semirigid aircraft. Following World War II he returned to Italy and was elected a Communist member of the Italian parliament.

The airship-builder Umberto Nobile was the first person to fly over the North Pole.

74. RICHARD EVELYN BYRD
1888-1957

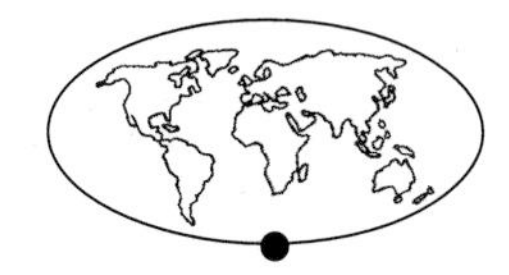

The first man to made extensive use of aircraft for polar exploration, **Richard Evelyn Byrd** was born in Winchester, Virginia and graduated from the US Naval Academy in 1912. He entered the aviation service in 1917 and became a pilot in 1918. During the remainder of World War I he was commander of the US naval aviation in Canada.

Byrd commanded the naval aviation unit of the US Navy expedition to Greenland in 1919, which was undertaken under the auspices of the National Geographic Society. In May 1926, he flew with **Floyd Bennett** from King's Bay, Spitsbergen to near the **North Pole** and back, a journey of 1,360 miles, completed in 15 hours. In a sensational flight from New York to France in 1927 with three other persons, he was forced down on the surf of Ver-sur-Mer after flying 4,200 miles.

Admiral Richard Evelyn Byrd.

In 1928 Byrd made his first Antarctic expedition and established his base, "**Little America**," on the Bay of Whales, Ross Sound, which is still a major research center. He was at the controls of the Fokker trimotor in the first flight over the **South Pole** in 1929. With him were **Bernt Balchen, Howard June**, and others.

While they were following **Roald Amundsen**'s route (see No. 70), they went east on the return and disproved the existence of Amundsen's suspected "Carmenland."

In this expedition, geological parties under **Lawrence Gould** were successful and work in biology, meteorology, and other sciences was accomplished by the party's large group of scientific personnel.

Byrd's second expedition to the Antarctic in 1933-1935 brought him again to Little America, and during this and the earlier expedition he made many important discoveries, among them Edsel Ford Mountains and Marie Byrd Land, which he claimed as United States territory. In 1934 he remained alone at a weather station 123 miles south of Little America from March to August. He became ill from carbon monoxide poisoning and was rescued by a party from Little America.

Both the 1928 and the 1933 expeditions were exceedingly well-equipped and highly successful. Byrd proved himself a prudent and capable leader. In 1939, Byrd went south as head of the US Antarctic Service, and made four flights, discovery of five new mountain ranges, a large peninsula, five islands and 700 miles of hitherto unknown stretches of Antarctic coast.

In World War II Byrd served on special missions in Europe and the Pacific and was adviser to the Commander in Chief of the Fleet and Chief of Naval Operations. In 1947 he led the Navy expedition to Antarctica, again flew over the South Pole, and discovered many new topographical features. He wrote *Skyward* (1928), *Little America* (1930), *Discovery* (1935), *Exploring with Byrd* (1938) and *Alone* (1938).

75. AMELIA EARHART
1897-1937?

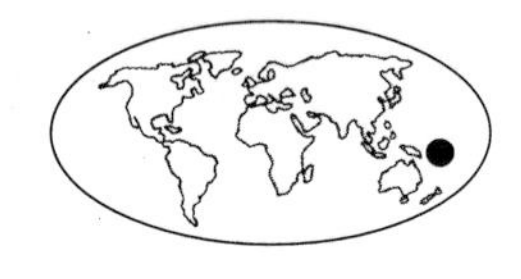

The early history of aviation is filled with the names of the men who pioneered this form of transportation, but there were many women who also contributed to the legend. Among them were people such as **Harriet Quimby** and **Katherine Stinson**, who were important early pacesetters. Perhaps the most important, for her high level visibility and her enduring legend, was **Amelia Earhart**.

Born in Atchison, Kansas, she flew as a passenger with Wilmar Stutz and Louis Gordon 2,000 miles from Newfoundland to Wales in 1928, becoming the first woman to cross the Atlantic by airplane. In the same year, she flew solo across the United States, becoming the first woman to do so.

In May 1932, Earhart made the first solo Atlantic flight after **Charles Lindbergh**'s historic feat (see No. 77), and the first ever by a woman, reaching Ireland in 13.5 hours. Congress awarded her the Distinguished Flying Cross, making her the only woman so honored until well after World War II. In 1935 she became the first pilot to make a solo flight over the Pacific, flying from Honolulu to Oakland, California. In 1931, she married George Palmer Putnam, a publisher and explorer.

Amelia Earhart.

By 1937, she was ready for her biggest feat to date, to become the first woman to fly around the world. All previous flights "around the world" were made by short cuts within the Northern Hemisphere. Amelia Earhart planned to circle the globe at its widest, close to the Equator.

On May 21, 1937, she flew out of Oakland in a specially modified Lockheed Model 10E Electra. She and navigator **Fred Noonan were accompanied as far as** Miami by her husband and mechanic Bo McNeely. From there, she and Noonan flew to South America, east to Africa, and then on to the East Indies.

On July 1, she and Noonan took off from Lae, New Guinea, flying over open water toward Howland Island, 2,556 miles away. Their last radio transmission was heard aboard the US Coast Guard cutter *Itasca* 20 hours and 16 minutes after they took off. The Electra never arrived at Howland and the pair of people were never heard from again. After an exhaustive, 17-day search undertaken by the US Navy and other vessels, no wreckage was found.

Earhart's disappearance became one of the most riveting mysteries of the twentieth century. It was supposed that the aircraft sank in deep water, but there were rumors of it being forced down on a Japanese-occupied island, and evidence discovered in the 1980s suggests that Earhart and Noonan may have survived for a time on a deserted island.

76. CHARLES LINDBERGH
1902-1974

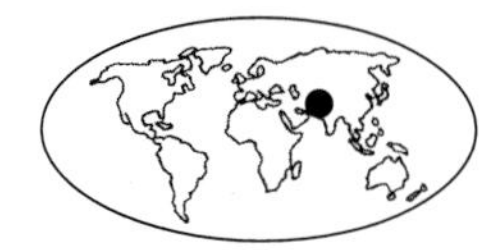

Charles Augustus Lindbergh.

The shy American aviator who captured the imagination of the world and became an overnight hero in 1927, **Charles Augustus Lindbergh**, was born in Detroit, Michigan. His family had come to the United States from Sweden in 1860 and settled in Sauk Center, Minnesota. Lindbergh's father and namesake served as a Progressive Republican in the US House of Representatives from 1907 to 1917, as an outspoken foe of trusts and war profiteers. The aviator's mother, partly of Irish descent, was a science teacher and encouraged his mechanical interests. Lindbergh spent his boyhood in Little Falls, Minnesota, graduated from high school there in 1918, and entered the University of Wisconsin in 1920 to study mechanical engineering.

After leaving the university without a degree in 1922, he took a minimum of flying lessons, and with a partner, he "barnstormed" circuses and fairs throughout the Midwest states. He bought a used airplane for $500 and in March, 1924, enrolled as a cadet in the US Air Service Reserve at Brooks Field, Texas. He was commissioned a first lieutenant in November 1925 and, in April 1926, made his first long-distance flight (from St. Louis to Chicago) as a US Air Mail Service pilot.

Lindbergh's dream was to be the first person to fly solo across the Atlantic. It was as much for the glory as for the $25,000 prize offered by **Raymond Orteig** for the first nonstop transatlantic flight from New York to Paris. "Lindy" secured financial backing, and acquired an aircraft, the monoplane *The Spirit of St. Louis*, built by **Claude Ryan** in San Diego. In turn he flew it from California to Curtiss Field, New York to establish a coast-to-coast record. On May 20, 1927, Lindbergh took off from Roosevelt Field to begin his flight across the Atlantic, alone.

The next evening he landed safely near Paris. After tremendous ovations in Europe, he returned to the United States in an American cruiser.

Few men had been accorded the laudation that Lindbergh, only 25, received then and in the years immediately following. Between May 21 and June 17, 1927, "The Lone Eagle" received 3,500,000 pieces of mail, numerous medals, and citations, and was promoted to colonel in the Air Reserve. The Guggenheim Foundation sponsored his air visits to 75 cities in the United States, and he made government-arranged good-will tours to Mexico, Central America, and the West Indies. His own story of his famous flight, *We* (1927), was a tremendous success and was often reprinted.

In 1929 Lindbergh became a consultant to **Juan Trippe**'s Pan American World Airways, and in 1929 he became technical adviser to the aeronautical branch of the US Department of Commerce. Also in 1929, he married **Anne Spencer Morrow**. They made a transcontinental record together in 1930, a transpacific good-will flight to the Orient, an archaeological tour over Central America, and in 1933, a trip of almost 30,000 miles during which they landed in 21 countries. After the tragedy of the 1932 kidnaping and murder of their first son, **Charles A. Lindbergh, Jr.**, and the merciless publicity which surrounded the trial in 1935, the Lindberghs moved to Great Britain. There he wrote *Culture of Organs* (1938).

Charles and Anne Morrow Lindbergh.

Shortly before World War II, Lindbergh returned to the United States, resumed his work for the Air Corps, and strongly urged American isolation and neutrality, incurring severe public criticism. He resigned his Air Corps commission in April 1941, after President **Franklin D. Roosevelt** called him a "copperhead" for his political activities. During World War II, as a civilian, he helped train Allied pilots, and developed techniques for conserving fuel over long ocean flights and for taking heavily loaded planes aloft from difficult airstrips.

After the war, **General H. H. Arnold** disclosed that Lindbergh was the man who first alerted top Air Corps officers to prewar developments in the German Luftwaffe, and convinced them of the need for sweeping modernizations of US combat aircraft in 1939. It also was revealed that Lindbergh had begun analysis of foreign warplanes in 1936, and that he made his unpopular visits to Nazi Germany at the request of US intelligence officers.

Lindbergh's tremendous prestige gained him an open-armed welcome by the Luftwaffe's Marshal Herman Goering, and his technical knowledge made possible the assembly of data which was described as an outstanding piece of prewar intelligence. After the war, he became an aviation consultant, and wrote *Of Flight and Life* (1948). He spent much of his later years at his home near Hana, on the Hawaiian island of Maui, which is where he died in 1974.

77. JACQUES-YVES COUSTEAU
b. 1910

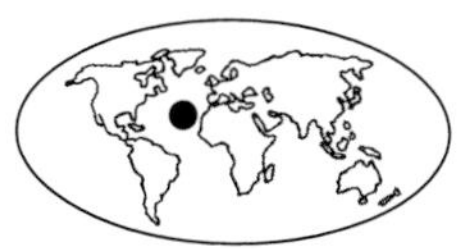

The most highly-regarded marine explorer of all time, **Jacques-Yves Cousteau** was born at St. Andre-de-Cubzac, France on June 11, 1910.

He was the founder of the *Groupe d'etudes et de Researches Sous-marines*, formed in Toulon, France in 1946, as well as of the *Campagnes Oceanographiques Francaises*, started at Marseille in 1950 and *Centre d'etudes Marines Avancees* (formally *Office Francais de Researches Sous-marines*). He led the scientific cruise around the world in 1967 that became the basis for the TV series *The Undersea World of Jacques-Yves Cousteau*.

Among his other important scientific expedition were those to the Antarctic and Chilean Coast in 1972, his expedition to the Amazon in 1982, and to the Mississippi River in 1983. His Rediscovery of the World project, a major ecological awareness effort, took him to Haiti, Cuba, the Marquesas Islands, New Zealand and Australia, beginning in 1985.

In the nineteenth century, the objective of exploration evolved from economics to science. In the twentieth century a new breed of explorer emerged, the ecologically minded documentary filmmaker, who recorded distant natural places visually. A member of this new school, Cousteau made a long series of undersea films, beginning with *The Silent World* (1956) which won the Grand Prix, Gold Palm Award at the Cannes Film Festival and the Academy Award for best documentary feature. *The Golden Fish* (1959) won the Gold Palm award at the Cannes Film Festival and the Academy Award in 1959. *The World Without Sun* (1965) won the Academy Award for best short film of 1965.

Meanwhile, his TV specials include *The Tragedy of the Red Salmon, The Desert Whales, Lagoon of Lost Ships, The Dragons of Galapagos, Secrets of the Southern Caves, The Unsinkable Sea Otter, A Sound of Sea Dolphins, South to Fire and Ice, The Flight of Penguins, Beneath the Frozen World, Blizzard of Hope Bay, Life at the End of the World* (film series), *Cousteau's Rediscovery of the World I* (1985-1991) and *Rediscovery of the World II* (1994).

Jacques-Yves Cousteau.

Jacques Cousteau has also written a number of books which, like his films, are around the theme of preservation of the world's undersea ecosystems. Among his books are *The Silent World* (1952, with **James Dugan**), *The Living Sea* (1963), *World Without Sun* (1965, with **Philippe Cousteau**), *The Shark: Splendid Savage of the Sea* (1970, with Philippe Cousteau), *Life and Death in a Coral Sea* (1971), *Dolphins* (1975), *A Bill of Rights for Future Generations* (1980), *The Cousteau Almanac of the Environment* (1981), *Calypso* (1983), *Amazon Journey* (1984, with Yves Paccalet) and *Whales* (1988).

Cousteau was also the co-inventor, with Emile Gagnon, of the **aqualung** in 1943; and with Malavard and Charrier of the **turbosail system** in 1985.

78. EDMUND PERCIVAL HILLARY
b. 1919

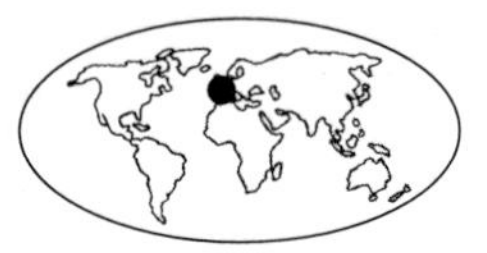

Known universally as "the man who conquered Everest," **Sir Edmund Percival Hillary**, was born in New Zealand, where he attended Auckland Grammar School and graduated from the University of Auckland.

During the Second World War, he served in the Royal New Zealand Air Force, flying Catalinas in the Pacific from 1944 to 1945. In 1951, he joined the New Zealand expedition to the Himalayas. He was invited to join the British reconnaissance over Everest under **Eric Shipton** and took part in the British expedition to Cho Oyu in 1952.

In 1953, he was a member of the British Mount Everest Expedition under Sir John Hunt.

Few sights on Earth inspire more awe than that great peak in the Himalayan Mountain Range, once known to British surveyors as Peak XV, and still known in Tibetan folklore as "the mountain so high that a bird can't fly over it."

Edmund Percival Hillary.

Known as "the top of the world," Everest is considered by most to be tallest mountain on Earth. Most sources, including the 1994 *Oxford Encyclopedic World Atlas*, list Everest at 29,029 feet.

When asked why he would want to climb the world's tallest mountain, Hillary replied with his now famous quip: "Because it's there."

Long considered unclimbable, Everest attracted an aura of foreboding from all the climbers who disappeared or died trying to scale it. The first successful attempt finally came after a climb of great difficulty, when Hillary and his Sherpa companion **Tenzing Norgay** reached the summit on May 29, 1953. Hillary was the leader of the New Zealand Alpine Club Expedition to Barun Valley in 1954 and the New Zealand Antarctic Expedition of 1956-1958. It was with this expedition that he reached the South Pole in December 1957. Hillary returned to the Himalayas as the leader of expeditions in 1961, 1963 and 1964.

Among Hillary's awards are the Polar Medal (1958) and the Gurkha Right Hand (1st Class).

Hillary wrote extensively about his experiences from the ends of the earth to the top of the world. His published works include *High Adventure* (1955), *The Crossing of Antarctica* (with Sir Vivian Fuchs, 1958), *No Latitude for Error* (1961), *High in the Thin, Cold Air* (with Desmond Doig, 1963) and *Schoolhouse in the Clouds* (1965).

The president of Voluntary Service Abroad in New Zealand since 1962, Hillary retired to Remuera Road, Auckland, New Zealand, where he was a bee farmer for many years.

79. JACQUES PICCARD
b. 1922

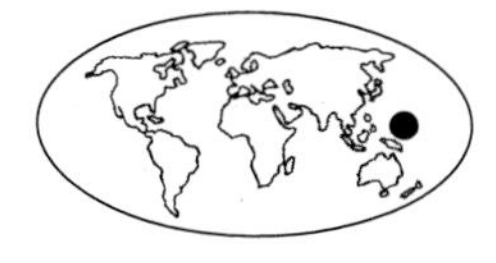

The Swiss scientist and bathyscaphe designer who helped make the deepest dive in history, **Jacques Ernest Jean Piccard** was educated at the University of Geneva and at the prestigious Institute Universitaire de Hautes Etudes Internationales in Geneva.

He was assistant professor of economics at Geneva from 1946 to 1948 and a consultant scientist to several American organizations for deep sea research. In the 1950s, Jacques collaborated with his father, Professor **Auguste Piccard**, in the construction for the US Navy, of the bathyscaphe *Trieste*.

With the US Navy's **Don Walsh** (see No. 87), Piccard conducted numerous underwater explorations, particularly in the **Challenger Deep** in the **Marianas Trench** of the western Pacific Ocean. On January 23, 1960, they descended for four hours and 48 minutes to reach a depth of 35,813 feet at 1:10 pm.

They found the water to be only five degrees above freezing, and the water pressure to be 16,883 pounds per square inch.

The information that they brought back about the flora and fauna at that depth was revolutionary and a dozen new species were discovered. This was especially important, because no one has been back. In the four decades since this epic dive, no human being has explored an ocean to nearly so great a depth.

Piccard went on to build the world's first tourist submarine, the *Auguste Piccard*. He made more than 60 dives in Mediterranean and Pacific, and has been awarded France's Croix de Guerre and the United States Distinguished Public Service Award.

Jacques Piccard.

80. ALAN SHEPARD
b. 1923

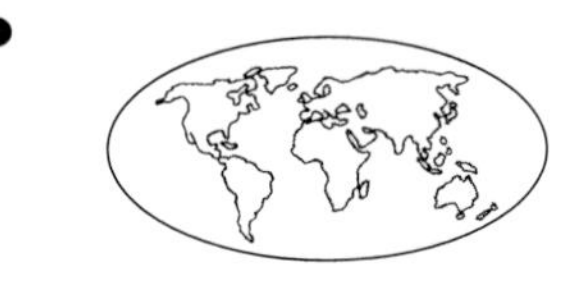

The first American to fly into outer space, and the fifth human being to set foot on the moon, **Alan B. Shepard** began his naval career, after graduation from Annapolis, on a destroyer deployed in the Pacific during World War II. He subsequently entered flight training at Corpus Christi, Texas, and Pensacola, Florida, and received his wings in 1947. In 1950, he attended the United States Navy Test Pilot School at Patuxent River, Maryland. After graduation, he participated in flight test work which included high-altitude tests.

He had logged more than 8,000 hours of flying time, including 3,700 hours in jet aircraft, when, as a Rear Admiral, Shepard was one of the Mercury astronauts named by NASA in April 1959.

On May 5, 1961, in the **Freedom 7** spacecraft, he was launched by a Redstone vehicle on a ballistic trajectory suborbital flight—a flight which carried him to an altitude of 116 miles and to a landing point 302 miles down the Atlantic Missile Range.

In 1963, he was designated Chief of the Astronaut Office, with responsibility for monitoring the coordination, scheduling, and control over all activities involving NASA astronauts.

Shepard made his second space flight as spacecraft commander on **Apollo 14**, from January 31 to February 9, 1971.

He was accompanied on mankind's third lunar landing mission by **Stuart A. Roosa**, command module pilot, and **Edgar Mitchell** (see No. 85), lunar module pilot. Maneuvering their lunar module, "Antares," to a landing in the hilly, upland Fra Mauro region of the moon, Shepard and Mitchell subsequently deployed and activated various scientific equipment and experiments and collected almost 100 pounds of lunar samples for return to Earth.

Shepard's mission aboard Apollo 14 is also remembered on a somewhat whimsical note for his being the only person ever to hit a golf ball on the moon.

More serious Apollo 14 achievements helped pave the way for future missions. These included the first use of a color TV with vidicon tubes on the lunar surface.

Shepard was appointed by the President in July 1971 as a delegate to the 26th United Nations General Assembly and served through the entire assembly, which lasted from September to December 1971.

He resumed his duties as Chief of the Astronaut Office in June 1971 and served in this capacity until he retired from NASA and the Navy on August 1, 1974 to enter private business in Houston, Texas.

Alan Shepard.

81. EDWIN "BUZZ" ALDRIN
b. 1930

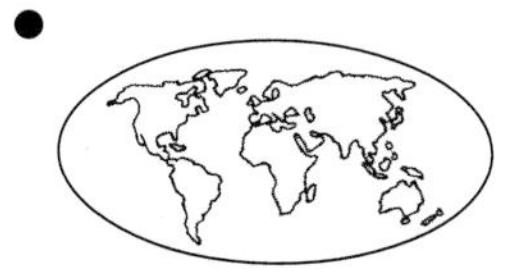

The second human being to walk on the lunar surface, Dr. **Edwin E. "Buzz" Aldrin, Jr.** was born in Montclair, New Jersey on January 20, 1930. After graduating from the United States Military Academy, he served as a fighter pilot in Korea, flying 66 missions.

After his assignment as Aide to the Dean of Faculty at the Air Force Academy, he attended the Massachusetts Institute of Technology, where he wrote his doctoral thesis on "Guidance for Manned Orbital Rendezvous." Following his Doctor of Science studies, he was assigned to the Gemini Target Office of the Air Force Space Systems Division in Los Angeles.

Buzz Aldrin in his Apollo space suit.

In October 1963, Aldrin was among the third group of astronauts selected by NASA. In 1966, Aldrin and command pilot **James Lovell** were launched into space in the **Gemini 12** spacecraft on a four-day flight which brought the Gemini Program to a successful close.

Because of a radar failure, the rendezvous with the previously launched Agena had to be accomplished for the first time using backup on-board computations, which Aldrin had formulated. He established a new record for extra-vehicular activity (EVA) by spending 5.5 hours outside the spacecraft. During the umbilical EVA, he attached a tether to the Agena and evaluated the use of body restraints designed for completing work tasks outside the spacecraft.

Aldrin was subsequently assigned as the backup command module pilot for **Apollo 8**, man's first flight to orbit the moon, where he significantly improved navigation star display techniques. With **Michael Collins** and **Neil Armstrong** (see No. 84), he was a member of the **Apollo 11** team that conducted the first manned lunar landing. Having landed in the moon's Sea of Tranquility on July 20, 1969, Aldrin followed Armstrong to become the second man to walk on the moon..

He left NASA in June 1971 and was the first Astronaut to return to active duty with the US Air Force. He was assigned to Edwards AFB, California, as commander of the Test Pilot's School.

Dr. Aldrin retired from the Air Force in March 1972 after 21 years of service. Since that time he has been an advisor on space shuttle proposals, a consultant to Inforex Computer Co., Mutual of Omaha, Laser Video Corporation, Amvideo Cable TV and Xonics Electron Radiology Company.

His best selling autobiography, *Return to Earth*, was published in 1973 and shown on network TV in 1976 starring Cliff Robertson. In the 1990s, Dr. Aldrin was serving as President of Research & Engineering Consultants, Inc., which he founded in 1972. He is on the Board of Directors of the Mental Health Association and was voted their National Chairman for 1974.

82. JAMES IRWIN
1930-1991

The eighth human to walk on the moon, **James Benson Irwin** was born March 17, 1930, and received Master of Sciene degrees in Instrumentation Engineering and Aeronautical Engineering from the University of Michigan in 1957. He graduated from the Air Force Aerospace Research Pilot School in 1963, and from the Air Force Experimental Test Pilot School in 1961.

Irwin was one of the 19 astronauts selected by the National Aeronautics and Space Administration in April, 1966. He also served as a member of the astronaut support crew of **Apollo 10,** and as backup lunar module pilot for the **Apollo 12** flight.

James Irwin.

Irwin served as lunar module pilot for **Apollo 15**, July 26-August 7, 1971. His companions were **David Scott** (spacecraft commander, see No. 89) and **Alfred M. Worden** (command module pilot). Apollo 15 was the fourth manned lunar landing mission and the first to visit and explore the moon's Hadley Rille and Apennines Mountains, located on the southeast edge of the Mare Imbrium (Sea of Rains). The lunar module, "Falcon," remained on the lunar surface for 66 hours and 54 minutes — a new record — and Scott and Irwin logged 18 hours and 35 minutes each in extra-vehicular activities during three separate excursions onto the lunar surface. Using "Rover 1" to transport themselves and their equipment along portions of Hadley Rille and the Apennines Mountains, Scott and Irwin performed a selenological inspection and survey of the area and collected approximately 180 pounds of lunar surface materials. Other Apollo 15 achievements included: the first use of a lunar navigation device (mounted on Rover 1); the first subsatellite launched in lunar orbit; and first extra-vehicular activity (EVA) from a command module during transearth coast. This was accomplished by Worden during three excursions to "Endeavour"'s external bay, where he retrieved film cassettes from the panoramic and mapping cameras and reported his personal observations of the general condition of equipment housed there. Apollo 15 concluded with a Pacific splashdown and recovery by the USS *Okinawa.*

On the flight of Apollo 15, Colonel Irwin logged 295 hours and 11 minutes in space — 19 hours and 46 minutes of which were in extra-vehicular activity.

On August 1, 1972, Irwin became the Chairman of the Board and President of High Flight Foundation, a nonprofit organization which he founded, that offers religious retreats and training activities.

83. CHARLES "PETE" CONRAD b. 1930

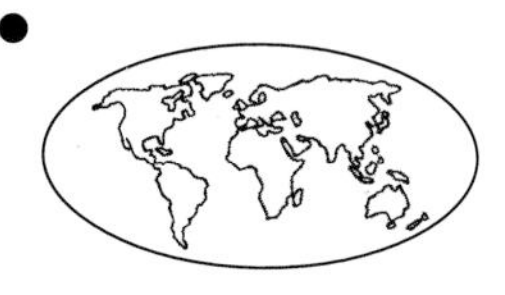

Charles Conrad, Jr., the third man to walk on the moon, entered the Navy following graduation from Princeton University and became a naval aviator. He attended the Navy Test Pilot School and ultimately logged more than 6,500 hours flying time, with more than 5,000 hours in jet aircraft. In August 1965, he served as pilot on the eight-day **Gemini 5** flight, and established a space endurance record of 190 hours and 56 minutes. In September 1966, Conrad occupied the command pilot seat for the three-day **Gemini 11** mission. He executed orbital maneuvers to rendezvous and dock in less than one orbit with an Agena vehicle.

Conrad was spacecraft commander of **Apollo 12**, from November 14 to 24, 1969. The Apollo 12 crew executed the first precision lunar landing, bringing their lunar module, "Intrepid," to a safe touchdown in the moon's Ocean of Storms and spent seven hours and 45 minutes on the lunar surface gathering geologic samples of the lunar surface for return to Earth, and completing a close-up inspection of the Surveyor III spacecraft.

As spacecraft commander on his fourth flight, Conrad flew the first manned mission to the **Skylab** space station, which launched on May 25 and terminated on June 22, 1973. With him were **Joseph Kerwin**, science-pilot, and **Paul Weitz**, pilot. Paramount to the completion of these objectives was deployment of a "parasol" thermal shade to alleviate the orbital workshop thermal problem created by loss of the micrometeoroid shield during the launch of the Skylab workshop. Also vital to the mission was a three-hour and 23-minute extravehicular activity by Conrad and Kerwin to deploy the jammed solar wing. Their success in extending the only remaining solar array system wing assured sufficient power for the conduct of the full 28-day mission, and would provide the needed energy to power the subsequent Skylab 2 and Skylab 3 manned missions. In logging 672 hours and 49 minutes each aboard the workshop, the crew established a new world record for a single mission. Conrad captured the individual endurance record for time in space by bringing this total space flight time to 1,179 hours and 38 minutes. Conrad has also logged 14 hours and 19 minutes in extra-vehicular activities.

In December 1973, after serving in the US Navy for 20 years (11 of which were as an astronaut in the space program), Conrad retired from the Navy to accept a position as Vice President, Operations and Chief Operating Officer of American Television and Communications Corporation (ATC) located in Denver, Colorado.

He was awarded the Congressional Space Medal of Honor (October 1978); two NASA Distinguished Service Medals; two Distinguished Flying Crosses and other awards. He was enshrined in the Aviation Hall of Fame in 1980.

Charles "Pete" Conrad.

84. NEIL ALDEN ARMSTRONG
b. 1930

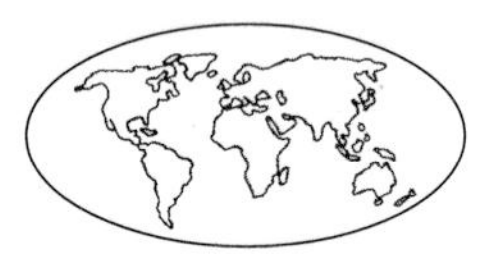

Neil Alden Armstrong was born in Wapakoneta, Ohio, on August 5, 1930 and received a Bachelor of Science degree in Aeronautical Engineering from Purdue University and a Master of Science degree from the University of Southern California.

Armstrong was a naval aviator from 1949 to 1952. He joined NASA's Lewis Research Center in 1955 (then NACA Lewis Flight Propulsion Laboratory. He later transferred to the NASA High Speed Flight Station (now Flight Research Center) at Edwards AFB, California, as an aeronautical research pilot for NACA and NASA. It was here that he flew the North American Aviation X-15 rocket research aircraft.

Armstrong was selected as an astronaut by NASA in September 1962, and he served as backup command pilot for the **Gemini 5** flight. In March 1966, flying with **David Scott** (see No. 89), Armstrong served as command pilot for the **Gemini 8** mission.

Neil Alden Armstrong.

He subsequently served as backup command pilot for the September 1966 **Gemini 11** mission, and was backup commander on the **Apollo 8** mission that orbited the moon in December 1968.

Armstrong was chosen as the spacecraft commander for **Apollo 11**, which was to be the first manned lunar landing mission. Launched on July 16, 1969, the missiion captured the imagination of the entire world.

On July 20, in an event that was to be one of history's first live, worldwide telecasts, the Lunar Excursion Module "Eagle," commanded by Armstrong and piloted by him and **Edwin Aldrin** (see No. 81), descended to the moon's surface and a successful touchdown, despite unexpected boulders in the landing zone in the Sea of Tranquility. The world held its breath until Armstrong calmly reported that "The 'Eagle' has landed."

Another historic comment came when Armstrong was the first human being to step on to the fine grey dust of the lunar surface. Armstrong quipped that it was "one small step for man . . . one giant leap for mankind."

The "Eagle" and its crew spent a total of 21 hours and 36 minutes on the moon, and Armstrong and Aldrin collected samples up to 300 feet from the initial landing site.

Apollo 11 returned to Earth on July 24, having changed history. The human race, who had reached the poles of their own planet only six decades before, had now set foot on another body in the Solar System.

It was the first of six successful lunar landings, but Armstrong's final space flight. He left NASA in 1971 to become a professor at the University of Cincinnati, where he taught engineering until 1980.

85. EDGAR MITCHELL
b. 1930

Edgar Dean Mitchell, the sixth human to set foot on the moon, entered the Navy in 1952 and completed his basic training at the San Diego Recruit Depot. In May 1953, after completing instruction at the Officers' Candidate School at Newport, Rhode Island, he was commissioned as an ensign. He completed flight training in July 1954 at Hutchinson, Kansas, and subsequently was assigned to Patrol Squadron 29 deployed to Okinawa.

From 1957 to 1958, he flew A-3 aircraft while assigned to Heavy Attack Squadron Two deployed aboard the USS *Bon Homme Richard* and USS *Ticonderoga.* He was a research project pilot with Air Development Squadron Five until 1959. His assignment from 1964 to 1965 was as Chief, Project Management Division of the Navy Field Office, for the US Air Force **Manned Orbiting Laboratory (MOL)** project.

Mitchell was in the group selected for astronaut training in April 1966. He served as a member of the astronaut support crew for **Apollo 9**, and as backup lunar module pilot for **Apollo 10**.

He completed his first space flight as lunar module Pilot on **Apollo 14** between January 31 and February 9, 1971. With him on mankind's third lunar landing mission were **Alan Shepard** (see No.80), the spacecraft commander, and **Stuart A. Roosa**, command module pilot. The mission represented the largest payload placed in lunar orbit to date.

Maneuvering their lunar module, "Antares," to a landing in the Fra Mauro region of the moon, Shepard and Mitchell subsequently deployed and activated various scientific equipment and experiments and collected almost 100 pounds of lunar samples. Mitchell was instrumental in the deployment of the Mobile Equipment Transporter, which was deployed for the first time on Apollo 14.

Mitchell also covered the longest distance travelled on the moon to date and was outside the spacecraft on the surface for over nine hours. Back in lunar orbit, Mitchell as landing module pilot conducted the first manned lunar orbit rendezvous.

Mitchell was subsequently designated to serve as backup lunar module pilot for **Apollo 16**, but Apollo 14 was his last space flight. After his retirement from the astronaut corps, he went on to serve as Chairman of the Board for Forecast Systems of Provo, Utah, and West Palm Beach, Florida.

Edgar Mitchell.

86. JOHN YOUNG
b. 1930

The ninth person to walk on the moon and the first commander of a **Space Shuttle** mission, **John W. Young** was also the only American to fly in space more than four times during the first 30 years of human space flight. On two of his *six* space flights, he commanded the Space Shuttle *Columbia*, and he visited the moon twice during the Apollo program. He and **Gene Cernan** (see No. 91) were also the only people to walk on the moon after first having visited it on an orbital mission.

As a test pilot assigned to the Naval Air Test Center, he set several important records in high-performance jets. In September 1962, Young was selected as an astronaut. His first flight was with **Gus Grissom** in **Gemini 3**, the first manned Gemini mission in March 1965. On **Gemini 10** in July 1966, Young, as commander, and **Mike Collins**, as pilot, completed a dual rendezvous with two Agena target vehicles.

John Young.

On his third flight, May 18-26, 1969, Young was the command module pilot of **Apollo 10. Tom Stafford** and **Gene Cernan** were also on this mission, which orbited the moon and completed a lunar rendezvous.

His fourth space flight, **Apollo 16**, April 16-27, 1972, was a lunar exploration mission, with Young as spacecraft commander, and **Ken Mattingly** and **Charles Duke** as command module and lunar lander pilots. Young and Duke set up scientific equipment and explored the lunar highlands at Descartes. They collected almost 200 pounds of rocks and drove nearly 20 miles in the lunar rover while on the moon.

Young's fifth flight was as spacecraft commander of **STS-1**, the first flight of the Space Shuttle *Columbia*, April 12-14, 1981, with Bob Crippen as pilot. The 55-hour, 36-orbit mission verified Space Shuttle systems performance during launch, on orbit, and entry. It was also the first time that a winged re-entry vehicle returned from space to a runway landing. Young's sixth flight was as spacecraft commander of **STS-9**, the Shuttle's first **Spacelab** mission, lasting from November 28 to December 8, 1983. The mission returned more scientific and technical data than all the previous Apollo and **Skylab** missions put together.

Though STS-9 was his last space flight, Young continued to serve as chief of NASA's Astronaut Office, with responsibility for the coordination, scheduling, and control of activities of more than 90 astronauts.

87. DON WALSH
b. 1931

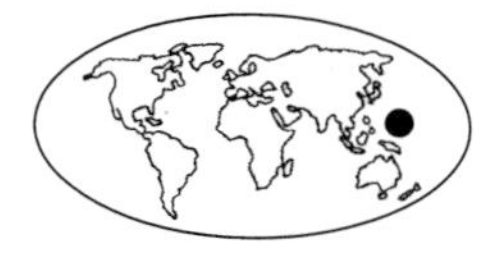

A member of the team that has achieved the greatest ocean dive in history, **Donald Walsh** was born in Berkeley, California on November 2, 1931, and graduated from the US Naval Academy in 1954, receiving a master's degree from Texas A&M in 1967.

As the naval officer-in-charge of the bathyscaphe *Trieste*, from 1959 to 1962, he and Dr. **Jacques Piccard** (see No.79) conducted numerous underwater explorations, particularly in the **Challenger Deep** in the **Marianas Trench** of the Western Pacific Ocean in 1960.

As discussed in the entry on Piccard, the two men descended to a depth of 35,813 feet, where the water was only five degrees above freezing, and the water pressure to be 16,883 pounds per square inch.

Having accomplished a expedition to "inner space" that has never been surpassed, Walsh went on to become director of the Institute of Marine and Coastal Studies.

He taught as a professor of ocean engineering at the University of Southern California from 1975 to 1983. He served as President and Chief Executive Officer of International Maritime, Inc. of Los Angeles and Managing Director of Deep Ocean Engineering, Inc.

He served on the boards of directors of the Center for Marine Transportation Studies at the University of Southern California, the Coastal Resources Center, the USN Museum Foundation and the National Advisory Committee on Oceans and Atmosphere, as well as the California Maritime Academy and as a trustee of the USN Underwater Museum Foundation.

As a strong advocate of maintaining an ecological balance in the world's oceans, Walsh is the author of *Law of the Sea: Issues in Ocean Resource Management* (1977), *Energy and Resources Development of Continental Margins* (1980), *Energy and Sea Power: Challenge for the Decade* (1981), *Waste Disposal in the Oceans: Minimizing Impact, Maximizing Benefits* (1983) and was the editor of the Journal of the Marine Technical Society (1975-1980).

Donald Walsh explored depths never before reached by human beings.

88. ALAN BEAN
b. 1932

The second man to fly a lunar landing craft, **Alan Bean** was the fourth man to walk on the moon. Born in Wheeler, Texas on March 15, 1932, he received a Bachelor of Science degree in Aeronautical Engineering from the University of Texas in 1955. He was commissioned as a US Navy officer upon graduation in 1955, completed flight training and was assigned to a jet attack squadron in Jacksonville, Florida. After a four-year tour of duty, he attended the Navy Test Pilot School.

Alan Bean with a lunar lander mock-up.

Bean was one of the third group of astronauts named by NASA in October 1963. He served as backup astronaut for the **Gemini 10** and **Apollo 9** missions, and was the lunar module pilot on **Apollo 12**, the second lunar landing. In November 1969, Bean and **Pete Conrad** (see No. 83) landed in the moon's Ocean of Storms—after a flight of some 250,000 miles.

They explored the lunar surface, deployed several lunar surface experiments, and installed the first nuclear power generator station on the moon to provide the power source. Captain **Richard Gordon** remained in lunar orbit photographing landing sites for future missions.

Captain Bean was also spacecraft commander of the second operational staffing of the **Skylab** space station from July 28 to September 25, 1973. With him on the 59-day, 24,400,000-mile world record-setting flight were scientist-astronaut Dr. **Owen K. Garriott** and Marine Corps Lt. Colonel **Jack R. Lousma**.

On his next assignment, Captain Bean was backup spacecraft commander of the United States flight crew for the joint American-Russian **Apollo-Soyuz Test Project**. Bean logged over 1,671 hours in space—of which over 10 hours were spent in EVAs on the moon and in Earth orbit. He flew 27 types of military aircraft as well as many civilian airplanes. He has more than 7,100 hours flying time—including 4,800 hours in jet aircraft. Captain Bean retired from the Navy in October 1975, but continued as head of the Astronaut Candidate Operations and Training Group within the astronaut office in a civilian capacity.

Bean resigned from NASA in June 1981 to devote his full time to painting. He said his decision was based on the fact that, in his 18 years as an astronaut, he was fortunate enough to visit worlds and see sights no artist's eye, past or present, has ever viewed firsthand. He hopes to express these experiences through the medium of art. He is pursuing this dream at his home and studio in Houston, Texas.

89. DAVID SCOTT

b. 1932

The seventh person to walk on the surface of the moon, **David R. Scott** was born on June 6, 1932, in San Antonio, Texas. He received a Bachelor of Science degree from the US Military Academy in 1954, standing fifth in a class of 633, and the degrees of Master of Science In Aeronautics and Astronautics and Engineer In Aeronautics and Astronautics from MIT. In 1962, he was awarded an Honorary Doctorate of Astronautical Science from the University of Michigan in 1971 and graduated from the Air Force Experimental Test Pilot School and Aerospace Research Pilot School.

His NASA career began with **Gemini 8** in March 1966, when he and **Neil Armstrong** (see No.84) conducted the first successful docking of two vehicles in space. Scott flew on **Apollo 9** three years later, an Earth-orbiting mission designed to test the craft for a future lunar mission.

Between July 26 and August 7, 1971, Scott commanded **Apollo 15** in the first extended scientific lunar exploration. Landing in the moon's Hadley Rille area, Scott and **Charles Duke** (see No.93) spent twice as much time on the lunar surface than any astronaut before them.

Scott went on to serve as director of the NASA Dryden Flight Research Center at Edwards AFB. After leaving NASA, Scott formed Scott Science & Technology, Inc., an advanced technology research and development firm.

As a pilot and astronaut, Scott has been awarded three NASA Distinguished Service Medals, the NASA Service Medal, two Air Force Distinguished Service Medals and the Air Force Distinguished Flying Cross. For the Apollo 15 mission he received the Air Force Association's David C. Schilling Trophy, the Robert J. Collier Trophy, the *Federation Aeronautique Internationale* Gold Medal for 1971, and the United Nations Peace Medal in 1971

An enthusiastic advocate of aviation, Scott is now a fellow of the American Institute of Aeronautics and Astronautics, the American Astronautical Society, and a member of the Royal Aeronautical Society and the Society of Experimental Test Pilots. He was also a member of the Board of Governors of the Flight Safety Foundation.

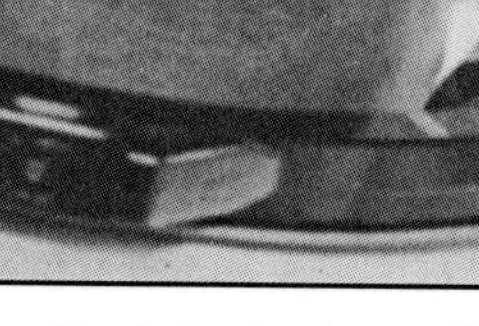

David Scott.

90. BRUCE McCANDLESS II
b. 1932

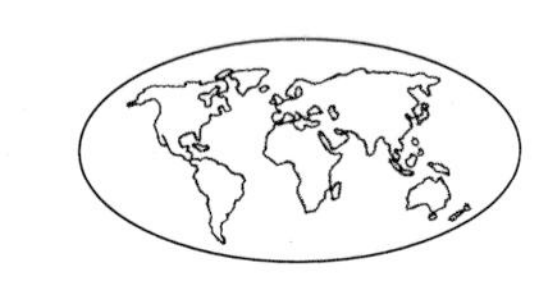

On February 4, 1984, **Bruce McCandless II** became the first human being to float freely in outer space without being attached or tethered to a spacecraft. He spent a total 11 hours and 37 minutes outside the **Space Shuttle** *Challenger*, four of the hours maneuvering freely, a "human moon."

McCandless graduated second in a class of 899 from the US Naval Academy and became a naval aviator in 1960. He logged more than 4,000 hours flying time —3,650 hours in jet aircraft.

Captain McCandless was a member of the astronaut support crew for the **Apollo 14** mission, and was backup pilot for the first manned Skylab space station mission in 1973. He was a co-investigator on the M-509 astronaut maneuvering unit experiment which was flown in the **Skylab** Program, and collaborated on the development of the **Manned Maneuvering Unit (MMU)** planned for use during Shuttle EVAs.

He was responsible for crew input to the development of hardware and procedures for the Inertial Upper Stage (IUS), Space Telescope, and the Solar Maximum Repair Mission.

McCandless was a mission specialist on the tenth Space Shuttle Mission (**41-B**), which was launched from Kennedy Space Center, Florida, on February 3, 1984 with a materials processing experimental module aboard.

McCandless was accompanied by **Vance Brand**, the spacecraft commander, Commander **Robert L. Gibson**, the pilot, and fellow mission specialists Dr. **Ronald E. McNair**, and Lt. Col. **Robert L. Stewart**. The flight accomplished the proper shuttle deployment of two Hughes 376 communications satellites. Rendezvous sensors and computer programs were flight tested for the first time.

During 41-B, McCandless made the spectacular first "flight" of the Manned Maneuvering Unit, and joined Stewart in performing two lengthy extra-vehicular activities involving the German Shuttle Pallet Satellite (SPAS) and the Remote Manipulator System (RMS). The eight-day orbital flight of *Challenger* culminated in the first landing on the runway at the Kennedy Space Center on February 11, 1984.

His last space flight was **STS-31** aboard the Space Shuttle *Discovery* in October 1990. After retiring from NASA, he joined the Martin Marietta Astronautics Company.

Bruce McCandless and the Manned Maneuvering Unit.

91. EUGENE CERNAN
b. 1934

The eleventh man to land on the moon, **Eugene A. Cernan** commanded **Apollo 17**, the last lunar landing mission in the twentieth century. A naval aviator, he was selected by NASA as an astronaut and flew with command pilot **Thomas P. Stafford** on the **Gemini 9** mission in June 1966.

On his second space flight, between May 18 and 26, 1969, he was the lunar module pilot of the **Apollo 10** mission to the moon with Tom Stafford (spacecraft commander) and **John W. Young** (command module pilot, see No. 86). Apollo 10 did not land, but conducted important tests and descended to within eight miles of the lunar surface.

In addition to demonstrating that man could navigate safely and accurately in the moon's gravitational fields, Apollo 10 photographed and mapped tentative landing sites for future missions.

Cernan made his third space flight as spacecraft commander of Apollo 17, the last scheduled manned mission to the moon for the United States. The mission was launched on December 6, 1972, with the first manned nighttime launch, and concluded on December 19, 1972. With him on the voyage of the command module "America" and the lunar module "Challenger" were **Ronald Evans** (command module pilot) and **Harrison H. (Jack) Schmitt** (lunar module pilot, see No. 94). In maneuvering "Challenger" to a landing at Taurus-Littrow, located on the southeast edge of Mare Serenitatis, Cernan and Schmitt activated a base of operations from which they completed three highly successful excursions to the nearby craters and the Taurus mountains.

During this last mission to the moon, the two men spent 22 hours walking on the surface. It was to be the longest manned lunar landing flight, lasting 301 hours, 51 minutes and the largest lunar sample return, with an estimated 249 pounds.

Eugene Cernan.

In September, 1973, Cernan assumed additional duties as Special Assistant to the Program Manager of the Apollo Spacecraft Program at the Johnson Space Center. In this capacity, he assisted in the planning, development, and evaluation of the joint United States/Soviet Union **Apollo/Soyuz** mission., and he acted for the Program Manager as the senior United States negotiator in direct discussions with the USSR on the Apollo-Soyuz Test Project.

On July 1, 1976, Cernan retired after over 20 years with the US Navy, and terminated his formal association with NASA. Cernan joined Coral Petroleum, Inc., of Houston, Texas, as Executive Vice President-International. His responsibilities were to enhance Coral's energy related programs on a worldwide basis

In September 1981, Gene Cernan started his own company, The Cernan Corporation, to pursue management and consultant interests in the energy, aerospace, and other related industries. He was also actively involved as a co-anchorman on ABC-TV's presentations of the flight of the Space Shuttle.

92. YURI GAGARIN
1934-1968

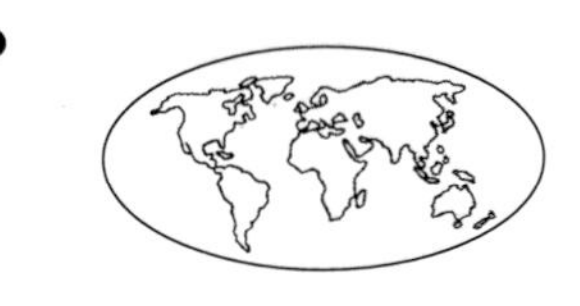

On April 12, 1961, the world held its breath to the news that the first human being had flown into outer space. Lieutenant Colonel **Yuri Alexeyevich Gagarin** was a Soviet Air Force officer and the Soviet Union's first cosmonaut.

Born in 1934, he was educated at the Lyubertsky Vocational School near Moscow, and at the Saratov Technical College. Starting out his working career as a foundry worker, he graduated as a Grade A pilot in 1957 and joined the Red Air Force. In 1960, he belatedly joined the Communist Party and later became a deputy to the Supreme Soviet of the USSR.

By this time, the race to put a human into outer space was on between the United States and the Soviet Union. The United States had an ambitious, heavily-publicized program. The Soviets had an equally ambitious, highly secretive program that was less cautious, but no less technically capable. By the spring of 1961, both sides were ready, but Gagarin's flight beat the American **Alan Shepard** (see No. 80) by a month. Gagarin flew in the spherical **Vostok 1** craft, nicknamed *Swallow*, which reached an altitude of 200 miles, orbited the Earth and returned safely to the ground near Smelovka.

The flight was hailed as a monumental achievement for Soviet technology and earned the young pilot congratulations from world leaders. After the flight, Gagarin was heralded as a Hero, First Class, of the Soviet Union and received the Order of Lenin. Also in 1961, he graduated from the Zhukovsky Air Force Academy and published *The Road to the Cosmos*.

Gagarin continued in the Soviet space program as it evolved with more and more cosmonauts making space flights. In 1968, he was scheduled to fly aboard one of the early **Soyuz** spacecraft missions, but he was killed on March 27 in the crash of a MiG-15U that he was piloting. The full details of the incident have never been fully explained.

Yuri Alekseyevich Gagarin was the first human being in outer space .

93. CHARLES DUKE
b. 1935

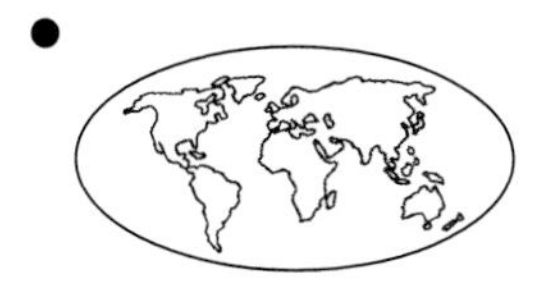

Charles Moss Duke, Jr., the tenth man to walk on the moon, was born in Charlotte, North Carolina, on October 3, 1935, graduated from the US Naval Academy and earned a master's degree in Aeronautics from the Massachusetts Institute of Technology in 1964. He served as a pilot in the US Air Force and was an instructor at the Air Force Aerospace Research Pilot School when he was selected by NASA as an astronaut in April 1966.

Duke served as a member of the astronaut support crew for the ill-fated **Apollo 13** flight and was the lunar module pilot of **Apollo 16**, which flew from April 16 through 27, 1972. He was accompanied on the fifth manned lunar landing mission by **John W. Young** (spacecraft commander, see No. 86) and **Thomas K. Mattingly II** (command module pilot).

Apollo 16 was the first scientific expedition to inspect, survey, and sample materials and surface features in the Descartes region of the rugged lunar highlands.

Duke, as landing module pilot, was responsible for setting the lunar module "Orion" on the Descarte's rugged Cayley Plains. He and Young then conducted a their record-setting lunar surface stay of 71 hours and 14 minutes.

In their first venture out of Orion, they spent over seven hours. In three subsequent excursions onto the lunar surface, they each logged 20 hours and 15 minutes in extravehicular activities involving the emplacement and activation of scientific equipment and experiments.

They collected of nearly 213 pounds of rock and soil samples, and Duke drove the Rover-2 nearly nine miles over the roughest and bleakest surface yet encountered on the moon.

In December 1972, Duke was chosen to stand by as the backup lunar module pilot for the Apollo 17 mission, which was to be the last of the Apollo manned missions to the moon.

In December 1975, with the Apollo program having come to a close, so in December of that year, Duke, who was now an air force general, retired from the Astronaut program to enter private business. He became a partner in Duke Invest-ments, and president of Southwest Wilderness Art, Inc.

Charles Duke.

94. HARRISON "JACK" SCHMITT

b. 1935

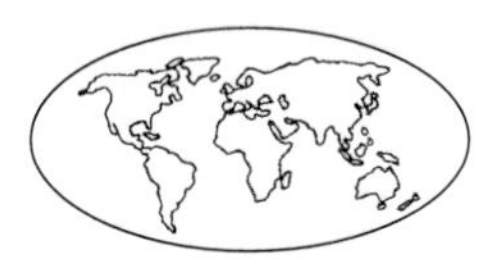

Harrison "Jack" Schmitt.

The only professional geologist to visit the lunar surface, **Harrison "Jack" Schmitt** was also the last of 12 persons to travel to the moon in the twentieth century. He trained as a geologist and scientist at the California Institute of Technology, as a Fulbright Scholar at the University of Oslo, and at Harvard University, receiving his PhD in Geology from Harvard in 1964 based on earlier studies conducted in Norway.

Jack Schmitt worked as an exploration geologist for the mining industry and the US Geological Survey before volunteering for the Apollo Scientist Astronaut program in 1965.

Before joining NASA, he was with the US Geological Survey's Astrogeology Center at Flagstaff, Arizona. He was project chief for lunar field geological methods and participated in photo and telescopic mapping of the moon, and was among USGS astrogeologists instructing NASA astronauts during their geological field trips.

After training as both a jet pilot and as a helicopter pilot and in the intricacies of space flight, he was selected as the Lunar Module Pilot and Scientist for **Apollo 17**, the last Apollo mission to the moon.

His studies of the Valley of Taurus-Littrow on the moon in December 1972, as well as his earlier scientific work, made Schmitt one of the leading experts on the history of the terrestrial planets.

After organizing and directing the activities of the Scientist Astronaut Office and of the Energy Program Office for NASA in 1973-1975, Schmitt fulfilled a long-standing goal by entering the political arena.

In August of 1975, Dr. Schmitt resigned his post with NASA to run for the United States Senate in his home state of New Mexico. He was elected on November 2, 1976, with 57% of the votes cast

Senator Schmitt was a leader in issues dealing with science and technology, energy, space missions and cost-effective defense, intelligence activities, health research and preventive medicine, education, deregulation, savings and investment.

In his last two years in the Senate, Schmitt was Chairman of the Senate Commerce Committee's Subcommittee on Science, Technology and Space and of the Senate Appropriations Committee's Subcommittee on Labor, Health and Human Services and Education. He went on to serve as a member of the President's Foreign Intelligence Advisory Board and the National Strategic Materials and Minerals Program Advisory Committee.

Schmitt continued to be an active proponent of technology development. As a consultant and lecturer, he wrote and spoke on a wide range of topics in the fields of technology, space biomedicine, geology and public policy.

He consults on the formulation of complex public and business policy issues a unique breadth of experience, ranging from the scientific to the practical and from the administrative to the political.

95. VALENTINA TERESHKOVA
b. 1937

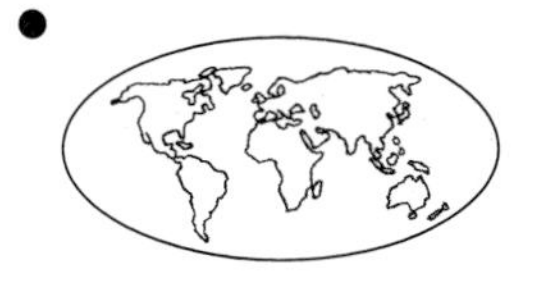

The first woman to fly in space, **Valentina Tereshkova** was born on a farm near Maslennikovo in Russia. Her father, a tractor driver, was killed in World War II before she was ten, and she went to work with her mother and sister in a cotton mill after working for a while in a tire factory.

She eventually joined the young communist league and in 1959, she took up skydiving, the first step on the ladder to space flight.

In 1961, the veteran of 126 parachute jumps, she joined the Soviet cosmonaut training program, which was then actively recruiting women. She trained for two years before being picked to fly aboard the **Vostok 6** mission in a capsule nicknamed *Sea Gull.*

The first woman and the twelfth person to fly in space, Tereshkova was launched on June 16, 1963 while **Vostok 5**, with **Valeri Bykovsky,** was still in orbit. Her Vostok 6 capsule completed 48 orbits over three days, for a total of 1,225,000 miles. She returned to Earth in "pitiful condition," for her training had not prepared her for long-duration weightlessness. Nevertheless, she was heralded as a Hero of the Soviet Union and received the Order of Lenin.

The Soviet space program discontinued the notion of women in space after Vostok 6, and it would be 19 years later that another female cosmonaut, **Svetlana Savitskaya,** would fly. From 1983 on, the United States began sending large numbers of female astronauts into space.

Later in 1963, Tereshkova married fellow cosmonaut **Andrian Nikolayev,** and their daughter Yelena was born a year later.

Although she would never again travel in space, Tereshkova continued her career as an aerospace engineer. In 1977, she chaired the Soviet Women's Committee, and in 1987 she became head of the Union of Soviet Societies for Friendship with Foreign Countries.

In 1963, Valentina Tereshkova became the first woman to fly in space.

96. REINHOLD MESSNER
b. 1944

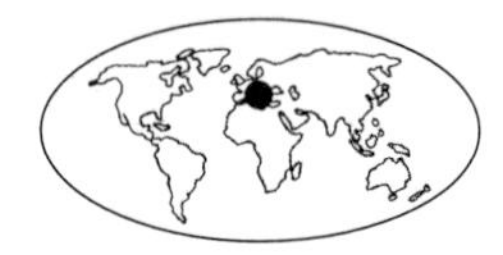

The most accomplished mountain climber in human history, **Reinhold Messner** was the only person to climb all 14 of the world's mountains that are over 26,250 feet without carrying oxygen. Born on September 17, 1944 in the Italian Tyrol, he was five when he climbed his first 10,000-foot peak in the Geisler mountains of the Dolomites, accompanied by his parents and older brother. In 1965 he climbed the north wall of the 12,802-foot Ortler, the highest peak in the eastern Alps.

Reinhold Messner.

Having conducted over 500 climbs in the Alps of Switzerland, Italy, France and Germany, Messner headed the South Tyrolean expedition to the Andes mountains in early 1974.

He made a successful solo climb of the 10,000-foot south face of the 22,834-foot Aconcagua in Argentina, the highest peak on Earth outside of Central Asia. Later that year he and **Peter Habeler** climbed the Eiger north wall in Switzerland in the record time of ten hours.

Motivated by his experiences with the Hunzas and the people of Nepal, Messner wrote *Bergvalker der Erd: Ehe Ihre Spur Verweht (Mountain Peoples of the World: Before Their Tracks Fade Away*, 1975).

In 1975, Messner was part of the Italian Alpine Club expedition to climb the 27,890-foot Lhotse, one of the peaks of the south **Mount Everest** massif. Heavy snows led to a change of plans, and most of the team dropped out.

However, Messner and Peter Habeler climbed the north wall of the 26,470-foot "Hidden Peak" in the Karakoram range without fixed ropes, high-altitude camps, native porters, or oxygen. In 1976, Messner made the first ascent of "the wall of the midnight sun" on Mount McKinley in Alaska In 1978 Messner and Habeler climbed the summit of 29,028-foot Mount Everest, the world's highest mountain, via the southeast ridge used by **Sir Edmund Hillary** (see No. 76) and **Tenzing Norgay.** Three months after his Everest climb, Messner climbed Nanga Parbat on its formidable western face, alone. In 1979, accompanied by the Bavarian mountaineer Michael Dacher, Messner (again without oxygen) climbed the second tallest mountain in the world, 28,250-foot K-2 (Godwin Austen) in five days.

Messner completed his goal of climbing the world's 14 tallest peaks in 1982 with his conquest of *Kanchenjunga.* Once called "a madman possessed by demons," Messner continued to climb, to write books about his experiences and teach climbing at his Alpinschule Sudtirol in Villnoss, Italy.

97. VLADIMIR TITOV
b. 1947

Born on New Year's Day, 1947, in what was then the Soviet Union, **Vladimir Georgievich Titov** had a long and varied career as a cosmonaut, including the experience of being a crewman on the longest space flight ever completed.

Having graduated from the Higher Air Force College in Chernigov, Ukraine in 1970, Titov became a pilot in the Soviet Air Force, flying MiG high-performance aircraft. In 1976, he joined the Soviet cosmonaut team and made his first space flight in April 1983. It was a two-day mission aboard **Soyuz T-8** with **Gennadi Strekalov** and **Alexander Serebrov**. Titov and Strekalov were scheduled to make another space flight a few months later, on September 27, 1983. During the launch of their **Soyuz 10**, sensors detected a malfunction and fired their escape tower 20 seconds into the mission, saving them from destruction as the rocket exploded.

Vladimir Titov in 1995, just before STS-63.

In 1987, Titov graduated from the Yuri Gagarin Air Force Academy, and on December 21, 1987, he and Azerbajani Flight Engineer **Musa Khiramanovich Manarov** (b. 1951) went into space aboard **Soyuz TM-4**. They docked with the Mir space station and went aboard for what was to be the longest human spaceflight ever, lasting 365 days, 22 hours and 40 minutes.

Musa Khiramanovich Manarov.

In 1990-1991, Manarov extended his time in space to a total of 541 days; the greatest number of hours for anyone ever. In October 1992, Titov and **Sergei Krikalev** became the first cosmonauts to undergo Space Shuttle training at NASA's Johnson Space Center near Houston, and in February 1995, he flew aboard **Space Shuttle** mission **STS-63**.

During STS-63, the Shuttle *Discovery* rendezvoused with the formerly-Soviet, now-Russian, Mir space station, Titov's home for a year of his life. This mission brought Vladimir Titov's total time in space to 376 days.

98. SALLY RIDE
b. 1951

The first American woman in space, **Sally K. Ride** was an inspiration to a whole generation of young women interested in exploration. Born on May 26, 1951 in Los Angeles. She received from Stanford University a Bachelor of Science in Physics and a Bachelor of Arts in English in 1973, and Masters and Doctorate degrees in Physics in 1975 and 1978, respectively.

Dr. Ride was selected as an astronaut candidate by NASA in January 1978. In August 1979, she completed a one-year training and evaluation period, making her eligible for assignment as a mission specialist on future **Space Shuttle** flight crews. She subsequently performed as an on-orbit capsule communicator (CAPCOM) on the **STS-2** and **STS-3** missions.

Her historic first space flight came when she flew aboard the Space Shuttle *Challenger* as a mission specialist on **STS-7**, which was launched from Kennedy Space Center, Florida, on June 18, 1983. She was accompanied by Captain **Robert Crippen** (spacecraft commander), Captain **Frederick Hauck** (pilot), and fellow mission specialists Colonel **John Fabian** and Dr. **Norman Thagard.** This was the second flight for the Orbiter *Challenger* and the first mission with a five-person crew.

Sally Ride went on to serve as a mission specialist on **STS 41-G**, which was launched from Kennedy Space Center, Florida, on October 5, 1984.

This was the largest crew to fly to date and included Captain Robert Crippen (spacecraft commander), Captain **Jon McBride** (pilot), fellow mission specialists Dr. **Kathryn Sullivan** and Commander **David Leestma**, as well as two payload specialists, Commander **Marc Garneau** and **Paul Scully-Power**. Their 197-hour mission conducted scientific observations of the Earth with the OSTS-3 pallet and the Large Format Camera.

Dr. Sally Ride.

In June 1985 Dr. Ride was assigned to serve as a mission specialist on **STS-61**, but she terminated mission training in January 1986 in order to serve as a member of the Presidential Commission on the Space Shuttle *Challenger* accident. Upon completion of the investigation she was assigned to NASA Headquarters as Special Assistant to the Administrator for long range and strategic planning.

Her children's book, *To Space and Back*, which describes her experiences in space, received the Jefferson Award for Public Service, and was twice awarded the National Spaceflight Medal. She is also the author of *Voyager: An Adventure to the Edge of the Solar System* and *The Third Planet: Exploring the Earth from Space*. In 1989, she joined the faculty at the University of California, San Diego, as a physics professor. She is also Director of the California Space Institute, a research institute of the University of California.

99.100. JEANA YEAGER and DICK RUTAN b. 1952, b. 1938

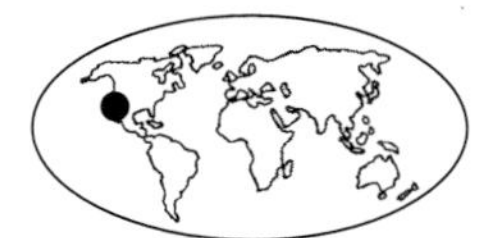

Until December 23, 1986, when **Jeana Yeager, Dick Rutan** and their aircraft, the *Voyager*, arrived at Edwards AFB, California, no one had ever piloted an aircraft around the world without stopping or without being refuelled in flight. In 1947 and again in 1957, the US Air Force had sent bombers around the world, but they were helped by aerial refuelling.

Jeana Yeager was a quiet Texan who grew up training horses. She studied drafting in community college, worked on a project to build a commercial space rocket, and later became a helicopter pilot.

Jeana Yeager.

Dick Rutan was a former fighter pilot, who worked as chief test pilot for Rutan Aircraft in Mojave, California, the leading-edge aircraft development company founded by his brother, the legendary **Burt Rutan.** The two met one another and became inseparable. In about 1981, Yeager suggested that they try to break the existing aircraft distance record (set in 1962 by a B-52 bomber flying 12,532 miles). Burt Rutan was sure that he could design an airplane that could fly twice that far, 26,000 miles, around the world. By 1984 the *Voyager* was nearly complete, incorporating a pioneering aeronautical design and the most advanced structural materials available. It had to be very light, but be able to carry all the fuel needed far a 'round-the-world flight.

Dick Rutan.

In July 1986, Dick Rutan and Jeana Yeager made a four-and-a-half day flight that set new world records for distance and endurance. Travelling in laps up and down the California coast, they went 11,600 miles. After several other extended flights they took off on December 14, 1986. Flying over the Pacific they almost ran into a typhoon, and over the Indian Ocean and Africa, they had to climb to less fuel-efficient altitudes to avoid storms.

Despite the cramped quarters, in which neither pilot could stand and nether could sit, the exhausted duo persevered, arriving in California ahead of schedule.

Jeana Yeager and Dick and Burt Rutan were awarded the Presidential Citizens Medal by then-President Ronald Reagan. Their book *Voyager*, was published in 1987. The airplane itself was donated to the Smithsonian Institution's National Air and Space Museum in Washington, DC. Jeana Yeager and Dick Rutan still live in a small house in Mojave.

TRIVIA QUIZ

1. What twentieth century mariner proved that a sixth century Irish saint may have been the first European to set foot in North America?
See Number 3.

2. What father and son called an ice-covered island "Greenland" in a scheme to encourage settlers?
See Numbers 4 and 5.

3. What Venetian sea captain was the first man to plant the English flag on the North American continent?
See Number 10.

4. What German geographer named the Western Hemisphere after the wrong explorer and later tried in vain to get America renamed "Columbia?"
See Number 13.

5. What Portuguese navigator discovered the island (which is named for him) that is the most remote inhabited place on Earth?
See Number 17.

6. Columbus tried and failed to reach the East Indies by sailing *west*. Who was the first European to reach the East Indies by sailing *east*?
See Number 18.

7. Who was the first European to reach the East Indies by sailing *west?*
See Number 22.

8. Who was the first European to lead an expedition to the shores of the Pacific Ocean?
See Number 22.

9. What Spanish explorer led the first major European expedition into the American Southwest in a vain attempt to find the seven golden cities known as Cibola?
See Number 27.

10. Who was the English sea captain who spent a winter near San Francisco Bay without ever actually finding it, and who compelled the Native Americans to crown him "King of California."
See Number 30.

11. What English explorer, sailing for the Dutch, was abandoned in the Arctic by mutineers and never seen again.
See Number 33.

12. Who was the first to sail *eastward* around the world?
See Number 43.

13. Who was the former presidential secretary turned territorial governor who died under mysterious circumstances, but who is best remembered for heading a scientific and geographical survey of the American West?
See Number 47.

14. What American explorer was jailed by the Spanish in Mexico and later killed by the British in Canada?
See Number 49.

15. Who was the first man to lead an expedition that confirmed the existence of the Northwest Passage, but who died before he realized what he'd accomplished?
See Number 50.

16. What American naval officer and Antarctic explorer inadvertently embarrassed the Lincoln administration during the Civil War by seizing a Confederate ship with British diplomats aboard?
See Number 52.

17. What French explorer discovered the fabled emerald mines of Jebel Zubara in North Africa?
See Number 53.

18. What Scottish missionary-turned-explorer won a reputation for being the first European to extensively explore the heart of the African continent?
See Number 58.

19. What American military officer, sent to explore the Far West, took part in California's brief war of independence against Mexico?
See Number 59.

20. What Irish explorer was the first to lead an expedition from south to north across the Great Australian Desert?
See Number 60.

21. What British explorer of Africa and the Middle East was later accused by his wife of translating "pornographic" material?
See Number 61.

22. What explorer, working with which photographer, were the catalyst for the creation of Yellowstone National Park?
See Number 62.

23. What one-armed American Civil War veteran led the first official United States expedition through the Grand Canyon?
See Number 63.

24. What Welsh-born American newspaper reporter went to Africa in search of a good story and wound up being one of the most important explorers of the interior of that continent?
See Number 64.

25. Who was probably the first woman to circumnavigate the Earth in less than 73 days?
See Number 67.

26. What British explore froze to death a few days after discovering that Raold Amundsen had beaten him in a race to the South Pole?
See Number 68.

27 What two explorers set a record for deep sea diving that has stood for nearly four decades, and which will probably stand indefinitely?
See numbers 79 and 87.

28. Who was the twelfth and last person (and the only geologist) to set foot on the moon in the twentieth century?
See Number 94.

29 Who was the first person to climb the world's 14 tallest mountains without oxygen?
See Number 96.

30. Who were the first people to spend an entire year in outer space?
See number 97.

31. Who was the first woman to fly around the world non-stop?
See Number 99.

INDEX

INDEX

INDEX